"You may have heard the expression, "Those that do – do and those that don't – teach." There are many authors who have written books based upon theory, yet Willie Miranda has written a book based upon his actual experience. If you're looking for a down to earth, step-by-step and successful strategy to guarantee your success in the real estate business – look no further! Willie's hands on approach will guide you through the maze of confusion that shrouds this industry and give you the advantage of knowing a proven path to success!"

Rick DeLuca
International Real Estate Trainer

"I have personally known Willie Miranda for over 15 years and know him as one of the most professional and informed real estate leaders in America. Not only is Willie an all-star coach and mentor for his team, his agents and his staff, he also is a leader and coach for agents across North America, each of whom would write something similar if asked. Willie's never ending quest for knowledge and information along with his ability to implement new techniques and ideas take second place to none. If I were ever moving to the Capital Region of New York, there is no question about what real estate company I would use, it would be Miranda Real Estate Group."

Lester Cox, Broker/Owner
Tempe, Arizona

"If there's anybody that knows how to help you overcome business challenges, it's Willie. His journey literally started from the ground up. You can't find a more authentic blend of humility and bold leadership than you can in this guy! Follow his guidance very closely because he cares enough to share the truth and nothing but the truth!"

Danny Griffin, National Real Estate Coach and Trainer
Cape Cod, Massachusetts

"Willie Miranda is the real deal! He's sold thousands of homes and has spent years developing systems to make his Real Estate success repeatable and predictable through the ups and downs of any market cycle. Unlike many who hoard their secrets, Willie openly shares his time, talent, and insight with clients, competitors, and anyone who needs help to achieve the level of success he's attained. If you want to earn more money in less time with little stress, let Willie show you how to turn your Real Estate JOB into a Real Estate BUSINESS!"

Bob Zachmeier, Tucson, Arizona

"I have had the great pleasure of knowing, learning, and being coached by Willie Miranda for the past several years. He has done it all in the Real Estate industry; he has sold a billion dollars in Real Estate, has a profitable office, an award winning team, and much more. Willie has taught me cutting edge techniques on how to market, as well as how to keep an ongoing stream of repeat and referring customers. The marketing system and referral system Willie taught me has allowed my business to double and continues to increase month by month. Willie has a common-sense approach that you can implement immediately. Willie Miranda will help you get results and increase your sales and profitability. Thanks Willie!"

George Lorimer, MBA
RE/MAX Solutions, San Diego, California

"This book is chock-full of tips and tricks of our trade, but even more than that, it shows you step-by-step how to build a successful business in Real Estate. When times are good, it's easy, but what happens when it's not good? This book will show you exactly how to secure your business to weather the ups and downs of the market, build your wealth, and find balance with your business and your life. This is a must read for anyone in Real Estate or considering a career in Real Estate."

Melisa Hatfield
RE/Max Masters Millennium, Denver, Colorado

"Willie Miranda is by far one of the most giving and helpful individuals that I know. He has been my Real Estate mentor and coach for the past eight years. He has helped build my Real Estate career into a successful business—a business I am proud to run. I am now able to take weekends off as well as go on vacation without my cell phone! Thank you, Willie!"

Amy Coleman, Broker/Owner
Golden State Realty Group, Inc., Sacramento, California

"Willie Miranda hits the mark with his new book. Not only are his tips realistic and practical, but they work! Willie helped me double my business in one year. It's very unique that someone this successful is willing to tip his cards and help others. Thanks Willie!"

Ken Reiley
Keller Williams Realty, Rancho Mirage, California

"Willie is one of the truly great people and leaders in the Real Estate industry. His knowledge pool seems bottomless, and his direction has led to exponential growth in my business. Like all great mentors, Willie guides with a nurturing hand, and he is always available to try and raise the professional bar in our business."

Scott Gaertner
Keller Williams Northeast Realty, Scottsdale, Arizona

"I have known Willie Miranda for well over ten years. I am the lucky one who actually gets to call him a friend and mentor. Throughout this book, Willie provides an in-depth look into his thriving Real Estate business and career. He takes down the walls that most Real Estate professionals surround their "secrets" with because he knows that he will receive more than he gives. Willie will give you specific examples and insight on how to make your business thrive through systematic and strategic marketing to your client base. There are few others that

I would listen to and trust 100 percent in what they say and do. I have implemented what Willie has written about in this book, and my business is growing by leaps and bounds because of it."

Aaron Kinn, Broker/Owner

Kinn Real Estate, Keller, Texas

"After interviewing over three hundred top agents on my podcast and selling over six thousand homes myself, I know when an agent is feeding me clichés and ambiguities rather than pure and proven money making formulas. What Willie lays out here is an exact HOW TO in tripling your commissions in a third of the work hours!"

Pat Hiban

New York Times Best Selling Author of *6 Steps to 7 Figures, A Real Estate Professional's Guide to Building Wealth and Creating Your Destiny* and host of "Pat Hiban Interviews Real Estate Rockstars" Columbia, Maryland

"Willie's guidance has been a HUGE game changer for me. His insights and experience have been invaluable in transforming me from a transactional agent to a career agent."

Mario A. Velazquez

RE/MAX, Chino Hills, California

"I have learned a lot from Willie. His coaching not only helped me become the Number 1 Keller Williams agent worldwide, but it also helped me fulfill my dreams of opening my own Real Estate brokerage in 2011, which ultimately became the number one residential resale team in Ottawa, Canada. Thank you, Willie."

Paul Rushforth, Broker/Owner

Paul Rusforth Real Estate, Inc., Ottawa, Ontario

"I had the pleasure and privilege of meeting Willie Miranda over fifteen years ago. Some people talk about what's happening—Willie makes things happen. Having built his business from the ground up, he actively practices everything he teaches. I have been in the business for over thirty-three years, am a broker/owner of a team of sixteen and am able to use Willie's systems both as a training system for my team and also to personally grow my company. His products aren't a pie-in-the-sky-system that reels you in to spending more money; you can start implementing and making sales immediately with what he provides. There is not one person that cannot benefit from Willie's knowledge. Whether you're a broker/owner, on a team, an independent agent, a new agent, or a veteran, putting these systems into practice through his personal coaching will allow you to reach heights of success you never imagined possible. Thank you, Willie, for all you have done for me and my team!"

Dawn McCurdy, Broker/Owner
McCurdy Real Estate, Latham, New York

"When it comes to leadership and understanding how a coach can transform your Real Estate business, there is no one that I trust more than Willie. I strongly believe that a good coach can inspire, train, hold you accountable, and lead you to your ultimate destination—success. I have witnessed Willie doing this for the past twelve years in helping hundreds and hundreds of people. Study this book like your life depends on it; it will save you millions of dollars and years of failure."

Masoud Badre, Broker/Owner
Ottawa, Ontario

"Willie's Real Estate systems flat out work! For years I struggled to survive with only a handful of listings. I went from just seven listings on my own, to twenty-five, to now over fifty listings each year following

Willie's systems. I now have a strong, predictable business year in and year out. Thanks Willie!"

John Stevens, Real Estate Broker
PCS HOMES LLC, Watertown, New York

"Willie has been a mentor of mine for several years now. I always look forward to his advice and help. I think anyone that has a chance to learn anything at all from Willie should jump at the chance. Thank you Willie for everything that I have learned from you in the past several years."

Scott Jones
Upland, California

"Willie Miranda and his Real Estate team are the best in New York and the Northeast! Willie has a wealth of experience and information that he freely shares to get every seller and buyer the best possible results. Trust Willie. He's taken care of me. I know he'll take care of you!"

Frank Prindle
RE/MAX Allegiance, Alexandria, Virginia

"Willie Miranda was the first formal Real Estate coach I ever had. I hired him in 2008 because of his willingness to show me a hands-on approach of how he handles his business and clients more effectively. He's mastered the processes and systems that make Real Estate a career versus a job. He really knows how to take great care of his clients and his Real Estate agents. As I worked with him I realized very quickly that he was a great leader and a great listener. It is rare to find a leader that can stop and listen to your needs and wants."

Marcus Hinds, Broker/Owner
Walnut Creek, California

"I wish I had this book when I started selling Real Estate. It's a great blue print to success."

E. "Rick" Feldman,
Investors Team Realty, Inc., La Verne, California

"Willie is a professional, experienced coach. He always has time to help me and answer my silly questions. His dedication and professionalism makes him a great individual to deal with. He truly cares about everyone. I highly recommend Willie to anyone looking for a fantastic professional. Many thanks for your guidance. Your knowledge and experience are very valuable."

Heidi Shiraz
Richmond Hill, Ontario

"Willie is a true inspiration in business and in life. His knowledge and willingness to help fellow Real Estate brokers and agents succeed is genuine and second to none. My own success in the Real Estate business today is very much the model Willie has instilled in his business and emphasized in this book—that the basic fundamentals of building a successful Real Estate business are sales and marketing, operations, and finance. Willie definitely hits the bullseye when he reiterates, "The road to success is always under construction."

Len T. Wong
Len T. Wong & Associates, Calgary, AB, Canada

"I am really glad I had Willie as my coach. He really knows his stuff and was always there for help when I needed him. If you are looking for a coach, I definitely recommend seeing what he has to offer. You won't be disappointed!"

Harry L. Kimbrough, Associate Broker
RE/MAX Professionals, Gillette, Wyoming

"I have had the privilege of knowing Willie Miranda for over a decade. My association with Willie has been instrumental in the building of my successful Real Estate business. Willie has always shared everything that he knows, and he truly cares about the success of others."

William Watson, President
The Watson Team/ReMax Professionals, Denver, Colorado

"I have known Willie for nearly ten years. Upon meeting Willie, I knew immediately that he was a mentor and resource that would lead me to levels in the Real Estate industry that I had never achieved before. Since that time, I have quadrupled my business while actually reducing my work hours and spending more quality time with my family. Willie has an uncanny way of planting ideas within you and then holding you accountable to those ideas. It's that kind of leadership that will lead you to your next level, wherever that may be. Thanks Willie, I owe you big time!"

Ed Laine
Miller Lane Properties, Bellevue, Washington

"Willie Miranda is one of the best Real Estate Brokers I know who has built an amazing business from scratch and continues to grow his business each and every year. This AWESOME book has such powerful yet practical ways to grow your business; every Real Estate Agent should read it. Applying the success systems in this book will transform your business and your life."

Duane LeGate, CEO
Commissions Inc.

HOW TO *NOT* GET YOUR *ASS KICKED* IN THE REAL ESTATE BUSINESS

· · · · · · · · · · · · · ·

HOW TO *NOT* GET YOUR *ASS KICKED* IN THE
REAL ESTATE
BUSINESS

· · · · · · · · · · · · · ·

WILLIE MIRANDA

*A*dvantage®

Published by Advantage, Charleston, South Carolina.
Member of Advantage Media Group.

ADVANTAGE is a registered trademark and the Advantage colophon is a trademark of Advantage Media Group, Inc.

Printed in the United States of America.

ISBN: 978-1-59932-627-6
LCCN: 2015950085

This publication is designed to provide accurate and authoritative information in regard to the subject matter covered. It is sold with the understanding that the publisher is not engaged in rendering legal, accounting, or other professional services. If legal advice or other expert assistance is required, the services of a competent professional person should be sought.

Advantage Media Group is proud to be a part of the Tree Neutral® program. Tree Neutral offsets the number of trees consumed in the production and printing of this book by taking proactive steps such as planting trees in direct proportion to the number of trees used to print books. To learn more about Tree Neutral, please visit **www.treeneutral.com**. To learn more about Advantage's commitment to being a responsible steward of the environment, please visit **www.advantagefamily.com/green**

Advantage Media Group is a publisher of business, self-improvement, and professional development books and online learning. We help entrepreneurs, business leaders, and professionals share their Stories, Passion, and Knowledge to help others Learn & Grow. Do you have a manuscript or book idea that you would like us to consider for publishing? Please visit **advantagefamily.com** or call **1.866.775.1696**.

I dedicate this book to my two beautiful daughters, Christine and Julia, who inspire me each and every day and make me so very proud to be their dad. I also dedicate this book to my supportive and loving wife Shari. My life wouldn't be the same without the three of you.

FOREWORD

· ·

by Craig Proctor

International Real Estate Trainer and Coach

CEO and Founder of Craig Proctor Productions

Former # 1 RE/MAX Agent Worldwide

My humble career beginnings parallel Willie's in an interesting way. If you read both of our biographies, you might think that working as a janitor at a hospital is a necessary rite of passage for someone on the way to selling billions of dollars of Real Estate the way both Willie and I have. Like Willie, I remember how exciting it was initially, as a young man, to receive a steady (if paltry) paycheck from my first full time job sweeping floors and taking out the garbage at my local hospital, and I could have gotten stuck there. Like Willie, I didn't.

In fact, I've been fortunate to be able to inspire tens of thousands of realtors worldwide with my excitement and passion for the "Millionaire Real Estate Agent Maker System" I share, but there are many of my students who, in turn, surprise and inspire me, and Willie is one of those.

I always find it interesting that you can expose two people to the exact same education, and each will walk away with an entirely different outcome. That's because just as important as what the teacher teaches is what the student brings to the lesson: an open mind or a closed mind, prior experience that helps them connect or not connect, and personal knowledge or skill that helps them leverage or reject. It is very true that, "When the student is ready, the teacher will appear."

Teaching is a two way street, and I think the people who get the most out of life are those who see and indoctrinate themselves as both lifelong learners and lifelong teachers. Again, Willie is one of those.

When we met for the very first time at one of my SuperConferences almost two decades ago, I could see that Willie would be one of those who would wring as much from what I had to share with him as possible. Not only did he come with an open mind, but he also brought with him a flat refusal to fail and the important skill of lateral thinking. After all, I was a Real Estate agent teaching other Real Estate agents how to systematically grow profitable Real Estate businesses. To Willie's credit, he took exactly what I taught him not only to his Real Estate business but also to his insurance business. Both businesses thrived.

From his humble beginnings, Willie has become an unqualified success, and I'm proud to call him my friend. If success is your destination, Willie is an excellent guide. A decade ago, understanding how good it would be for my company to leverage Willie's skillset, I asked him to join my coaching team, and between now and then, hundreds of agents from across the country have benefited from Willie's knowledge, patience, and tenacity.

A key part of what makes Willie the very fine teacher he is stems from the fact that he continues to commit to learning. As much as he certainly already knows, he regularly attends the SuperConferences and Masterminds I hold each year, and while there, he gives as much as he gets.

As Willie points out in this book, the road to success is always under construction, or to paraphrase John Lennon—success is a journey, not a destination. So carve out some time to benefit from what Willie is about to share with you about your own success journey, and enjoy the ride!

TABLE OF CONTENTS

EARNING WHAT YOU WANT IN LIFE

Ever since I can remember, I wanted to be a state trooper. I was intrigued by every part of law enforcement: the uniforms, sirens, police cars—you name it. Instead I became a very successful real estate broker with my own real estate group. The journey from my boyhood dream to living a life I love as head of a thriving real estate business was hard fought and hard won, with many lessons along the way. My goal in this book is to share those experiences with you to ease your path to success in real estate.

I was raised in upstate New York. Both of my parents were hard workers, toiling at their jobs for many years. My father worked on the railroad as an electrician. My mother worked in a factory. They always provided us with food and shelter, but if we wanted extras like the most popular brand of jeans or sneakers, we had to go out and earn the money ourselves to buy them. My parents instilled in us the message that we had to earn the things we wanted in life.

One of my earliest memories growing up was a cold January night when the money was tight, and we were going through heating oil like water. Then we actually ran out of both oil and money. We had a small electric space heater that my mother plugged into the bedroom, and that heater kept us alive for about three weeks, until my parents had enough money for oil again. I have never forgotten the look of defeat on my mother's face, sitting in that one room with three cold boys for 21 long days. I know that the fear of failure produced by that experience is responsible for the accomplishments I have attained today. Success was my goal from that day forward.

Every job I worked from that point on taught me something. My first job was delivering newspapers. It taught me at an early age the responsibility of getting up in the early hours of the morning to make sure my customers received their papers by a certain time. At fifteen, I discovered how corporate America worked by taking a job at a McDonald's restaurant. I learned the value of training, systems, and marketing. I also grasped how those things worked together to create a consistent product. When I turned 17, I took a full-time job at a hospital. I did every lowly task from housekeeping and maintenance to cutting grass and snow removal, but my main duty was to collect trash and medical waste from all the floors and take them to the trash incinerator room. What I remember from that experience was that there was a man who had been working the incinerator there for thirty years, and he gave me the kick in the ass I needed. Aware that I still dreamed of being a state trooper, but also knowing I liked having this job because it afforded me a car and other nice things, he turned to me one day and said, "If you don't get out of here, you will be here for the rest of your life. Don't make the same mistake I made by not going to college. You need to get out and get your education." The fact was that I wasn't able to pursue my education, because I couldn't afford a four-year college.

One day, while working at the hospital, a college student working for the summer suggested I look into being a resident assistant at the State University of New York at Oneonta. After speaking with him, I realized that if my room and board were provided for, I would be able to cover the tuition by bartending every weekend until I got my four-year degree.

I graduated from SUNY Oneonta in 1991 and applied to the New York State Trooper Academy, passing with very high scores. I also passed the physical and fitness tests required, but there was a hitch. There weren't any openings available. The next academy training program was an eight-month wait, so I needed to find a job until then. I began selling life insurance with Prudential Financial Services. Within the first six months, I had made more money selling life insurance with Prudential than I would have made in a whole year as a state trooper. I decided to stay with Prudential.

I did very well as a sales agent, moving up to sales manager, then taking over an office of 23 agents in Saugerties, New York. I did so well with that office that the next jump for me was to relocate again. By then I was engaged to my now-wife Shari, and we decided relocating wasn't an option for us. We wanted to stay in the Capital District area to raise our family.

So I started a new office with Allstate Insurance in August 1995. I obtained a small loan through the Small Business Administration (SBA) and used money I had put aside for retirement to open the office. In that first year, I went from making substantial money at Prudential to netting only about $12,000 with Allstate because I was putting so much money back into the business. I had also maxed out my credit cards to help build that office at Allstate. Three years later, I had a new house, a new baby, *and* $125,000 in credit card and business loan debt. Truth be told, I panicked. All I can remember is a feeling of failure flooding over me that took me back to that cold night in January with my mother and brothers sitting around that heater.

In the vein of what doesn't kill you makes you stronger, I refused to go back to that room. I refused to fail. All I needed was to make more sales and income, so I took a part-time job on top of my full-time job. I got into the real estate business.

In 1998, I read an article in a real estate magazine by Craig Proctor, in which he wrote about how he was selling so much real estate every month without doing any cold calling because he had a different method on how to attract ready-to-act buyers and sellers. He actually had clients calling *him* instead of him calling *them*, so his business was more like reverse prospecting, which was intriguing to me. I went to one of his three-day conferences in Toronto, Canada, and it changed my life. I immediately wanted to implement all the marketing ideas I had learned. But the real estate company I was working for wouldn't approve it.

So I found myself at the proverbial fork in the road, and noting that Craig Proctor was at RE/MAX, I jumped to RE/MAX also and used a lot of the same principles that I had learned from him. But then I did something unique; I also started employing procedures and systems that I had learned in the insurance business.

The insurance business is all about residual income, repeat/referral business, and taking care of your customers. The belief is that if you provide excellent customer service, then your customers, in turn, will give you referrals. I applied those principals to my real estate business along with the systems I learned from Craig Proctor, and my business began to explode. I went from 13 home sales in the first year to 53 home sales the following year and was up to 77 transactions by the end of year three. With that money, I was able to pay off my debt and invest more money back into my insurance and real estate businesses.

In 2002, I decided to open up my own business because I didn't want to pay franchise fees to RE/MAX any longer. I only had five agents to start with, and we all did a lot of marketing—billboard advertising, newspaper ads, postcards, newsletters, and moving trucks. I went on television and radio to attract more customers. The next year we did more than 100 sales. The year after that, we did 200 sales. The year after that, my business doubled again. I was adding more agents who were coming to me because I was building a unique team. I was teaching and training my agents how to build their own business within my business, and that was the secret to my success. By teaching them how to build their real estate business and stay clear of the mistakes that I had made, they were able to get a much quicker start.

Throughout the years, my business kept growing. In 2006, I was named one of "40 Under 40" in the local Business Review publication, which was a great honor. That same year, Craig Proctor asked me to do some coaching for other broker/owners and real estate agents who had teams they wanted trained by someone actually in the trenches. By 2009, I was the number-one real estate agent out of 2,500 real estate agents in the Capital District. All this came about as a result of the systems and the team that I had built. Today, I have over 70 agents who work for the Miranda Real Estate Group, Inc.

When I left the RE/MAX franchise to open my own real estate business, I remember two brokers sitting down with me and telling me that I couldn't leave. Their point? No one knew who Willie Miranda was or what Miranda Real Estate would be, and I'd be out of the business in two years because I didn't have a big corporate logo over my head. Despite the odds, what happened was just the opposite. My business doubled and tripled over a short period of time because I was able to apply my energy and extra resources into marketing my company to where it is today.

Many of the real estate firms I know have their agents believe that it is the company they work for that makes them successful. Let me ask you: What percentage of sellers do you think chooses an agent based on the company that they work for? Most people guess 40 or 50 percent. In fact, the National Association of Realtors says the actual number is 3 percent. **Only 3 percent of people choose an agent based on where they work and the association that they're with.** So what sways their choice? It's actually very simple. People want to do business with people they know, like, and trust. Those are the big three: *know, like,* and *trust.* People choose an agent based on the agent's reputation and knowledge, not on the company's name.

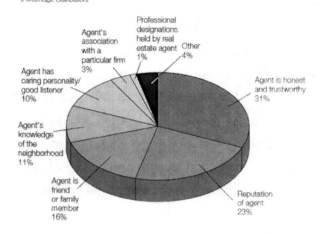

Exhibit 4-15 MOST IMPORTANT FACTORS WHEN CHOOSING AN AGENT
(Percentage Distribution)

Professional designations held by real estate agent 1%
Other 4%
Agent's association with a particular firm 3%
Agent has caring personality/ good listener 10%
Agent is honest and trustworthy 31%
Agent's knowledge of the neighborhood 11%
Agent is friend or family member 16%
Reputation of agent 23%

Your success or failure in the real estate business is in direct proportion to the number of people in your database who, when they think of real estate, think of you. Through this book, I want to show real estate agents how to build their brand, create a business, and have the same residual income and referrals that I have received over time. In order to build a successful real estate business, an agent must focus on three major components: sales and marketing, operations, and finance. The sales and marketing piece is all about building your database. The bigger your database, the more successful you're going to be. So in chapter 2, I'm going to show you how I was able to take my existing database, build it up, and keep my repeat/referral business coming in by staying top of mind. But it's also very important to bring new clientele into the database, and I'm going to disclose how to use marketing to bring new clients into your database.

The second component is operations. Just as I learned years ago in the food franchise business, it's imperative to have good processes and systems in place in order to run a successful business. In chapter

9, I'm going to share with you some of the different systems and tools that I've used and processes that I've developed at Miranda Real Estate Group to grow my company to where it is today. One of the main things that sets Miranda Real Estate Group apart from our competition is that we have first-rate systems in place, and our operations are fine tuned and managed by an outstanding staff.

The third sector is finance. In my work, I see a lot of agents who, when the market is good, are driving around in fancy leased cars and wearing expensive Rolex watches. But when the market is bad, I see many of those same agents out of business. In chapter 10, I will show you how I've been able to remain in my own world by managing finances well, by always having reserves and by being able to manage the fluctuating ups and downs of our sometimes-seasonal business. I want to make sure that agents know how to run their business, how to operate their finances so they don't owe $125,000 in debt like I did, and how to ensure that when things are going well, they are still putting money into a reserve account, paying their taxes, and building for their retirement.

The other thing I want to stress in this book is that there are two types of real estate agents: transactional agents and career agents. Transactional agents have no database. They have no systems or processes. Transactional agents tend to waste time, and they don't have any client loyalty because they go from one deal to the next. They don't keep in touch with their prior clients. They get leads from different sources, but they don't follow up with them or have systems in place to get the conversions they need.

Studies show that 80 percent of sales are made on the fifth to twelfth contact to obtain a customer. Most transactional agents will only call a lead once, maybe twice, and then will dismiss that lead as disinterested. Transactional agents are also what we call "ripe and rotten." They don't seek out additional training and/or education because they feel they already know everything. I also see a lot of transactional agents quit the business because they can't make it with the low profit margins that they have or because they burn themselves out working harder and harder all the time.

SALES STATISTICS

48% OF SALES PEOPLE NEVER FOLLOW UP WITH A PROSPECT
25% OF SALES PEOPLE MAKE A SECOND CONTACT AND STOP
12% OF SALES PEOPLE ONLY MAKE THREE CONTACTS AND STOP
ONLY 10% OF SALES PEOPLE MAKE MORE THAN THREE CONTACTS
2% OF SALES ARE MADE ON THE FIRST CONTACT
3% OF SALES ARE MADE ON THE SECOND CONTACT
5% OF SALES ARE MADE ON THE THIRD CONTACT
10% OF SALES ARE MADE ON THE FOURTH CONTACT
80% OF SALES ARE MADE ON THE FIFTH TO TWELFTH CONTACT

Source: National Sales Executive Association

Career agents use their time efficiently. They have their schedules down. They know exactly what their priorities are for the week. They are effective time managers. Career agents also know their numbers. They know the leads that they have coming in. They know what it takes to convert those leads. They also know what sales they have in the pipeline. They know how much they need to do in order to hit their goals throughout the year. As a result, they receive repeat/referral business because they're able to stay top of mind with their clients. They have good systems in place to not only take care of their clients before the transaction and during the transaction but, more importantly, after the transaction as well. A career agent also reads books like this one or listens to webinars or goes to conferences. They invest money on education and coaching to get them to the next level. They're continually seeking more knowledge and training. Because of that, career agents have higher profit margins and run successful businesses that they can turn around and sell or get a residual income from beyond their working years.

Transactional Agent	Career Agent
Tends To Waste Time	Uses Time Efficiently
Poor Spending Habits	Know Their Numbers
No Client Loyalty	Receive Repeat & Referral Business
Lead Squirrels With Low Conversion Rates	Systematic Database With Higher Conversion Rates
Ripe & Rotten – They don't seek additional training & education.	Green & Growing – Constantly Seeking More Knowledge & Training.
Low Profit Margins/Agent Burnout	Higher Profit Margins/Successful Business

The bottom line is that I want you to have a business that makes money but also allows you to have a balanced life. Transactional agents feel they can't have a balanced family life and a successful business because either they're home all the time with their families or they're always working and away from their families. Career agents believe there is a way to do both: to have a balanced family life and also have a successful business. My goal in this book is to show real estate agents across the country how they can do just that: have a successful life and a successful business.

I remember sitting in a Chinese restaurant several years ago with my family. My then-six-year-old daughter Christine liked to open up fortune cookies. She opened one and read it to me: "The road to success is always under construction." To this day, that quote has stuck with me, and I still live by it. I, who grew up afraid of failure, suddenly realized that you never really have success because it's always under construction. When I look back at the last 25 years of my working life, there have been many challenges and bumps along the way. But in order to achieve success, the challenges you face in your life must be overcome, and they will make you a stronger person moving forward.

I have a big sign on my office wall now that mirrors that fortune cookie. It reads: "The road to success is always under construction." It's the principle that I live by. In order to get what you want, you have to work hard in life, and you're always going to face struggles and bumps along the way, but as long as you keep your course and stay committed to your goals, you will overcome them. My goal with this book is to also help guide you to what you want to be: a profitable and kick-ass real estate agent.

CHAPTER 1

LEAD GENERATION: THE PILLARS OF SUCCESS

A nytime I sit down with an agent to talk about what his or her business looks like, I always ask what they are doing for lead generation. The agents I see struggling in the real estate business are usually the ones who don't have a solid, consistent method of generating leads. As I mentioned in the introduction, every business, including real estate, requires three major components (sales and marketing, operations, and finance) in order to be successful. If you think of your real estate business as a three-legged stool, the first leg must be sales and marketing, which is lead generation. Lead generation and marketing go hand in hand; thus, the sales and marketing leg of the stool is key to your business.

You need to start with a minimum of four lead generation pillars in order to have a solid foundation in your business. Think of the pillars as holding up the base of your home. If you only have three pillars supporting your house, it's bound to be a little weak. But by having all corners of your foundation covered, you have a strong base.

LEAD GENERATION PILLARS

| YOUR DATABASE | ONLINE MARKETING | OFFLINE MARKETING | GEOGRAPHIC FARMING |

The first pillar is your database. The more people in your database, the more business you'll generate. Your database should be a list of all your personal and business relationships. Include people who know, trust, and like you, as well as people you've done business with in the past. Your success or failure in the real estate business is in direct proportion to the number of people who are in your database and who will think of you when they think of real estate. It's that simple, and it's that important.

The second pillar is online marketing. Online marketing has grown tremendously over the past 10–15 years. According to the National Association of Realtors, in that time period the use of online marketing by buyers has grown from 74 percent to 94 percent. That's a substantial difference and an indication that online marketing is here to stay.

The third pillar is offline marketing. You can't neglect traditional and print advertising, because a percentage of your clients will not use the Internet or don't own a computer. You still need to market to them as well, and the best way to do that is through offline marketing.

The fourth pillar is geographic farming. This means cornering a strong geographic area in the market that you want to work diligently and consistently to get results that will pay off. You want to be known as the area expert and the "go-to" real estate agent when it comes time for them to buy another home or sell their current home.

Thus, database, online marketing, offline marketing, and geographic farming become the four main pillars of lead generation. Let's dive deeper into these pillars.

YOUR DATABASE

Develop your database to create a center of influence. I have my agents begin this process by listing a minimum of 100 people they know. I call it Project 100. The usual first response I get from agents is, "I don't know anyone," or, "I certainly don't know 100 people." In fact, statistics show that the average person knows 285 or more people—folks they are acquainted with in some way. You just might need a little help to trigger your memory for that list. Start by naming the current and past clients that you've served, not just in real estate, but in any prior profession as well, and dig down deep. You'll be surprised at how many people you can add to your database who still know who you are and who had a great experience with you. But since you haven't reached out to them recently, you may not be top of mind with them anymore.

Next take a look at the people you do business with on a day-to-day basis, whether it's your dry cleaner, a local restaurant or maybe a jeweler that you frequently use. These are people who should be added to your database and as a referral vendor for your business directory.

Third, consider your friends and family. Newer agents often say, "I don't want to do business with my friends and family until I sell a few homes and know more about the business." But if you have friends in your neighborhood and suddenly you see your competitor's sign go up on their lawn because they didn't know that you were in real estate and sold houses, you're going to kick yourself. This is exactly what happened to me early in my career, and it cost me a lot of money. Make sure the names of your friends and family members get into your database.

Finally, add your acquaintances: people who you cross paths with, people you went to high school with, people you know from PTA meetings or from your kids' sports teams. The best place to look for those names is Facebook or other social media sites. All of those people should be part of your database. Remember, the goal is to continually feed that database, while also deleting people who are not good prospects for future business.

There are several good software programs that can create databases for you. I currently use Top Producer, as it allows me to have all my contacts on my smartphone, iPad, and desktop simultaneously. If you're driving in the car, it will match up addresses to the mapping system that's on your smartphone. But you can also create a good database manually by using alphabetized index cards. The point is to develop some type of system, whether it's online, offline, or on paper.

It doesn't matter which one system you choose because, in the end, the best database is the one you *use*.

ONLINE
MARKETING

Create an online presence. As I said previously, 94 percent of buyers look online before reaching out to an agent. Some of the more popular search engines that buyers visit include Zillow.com, Trulia. com, or Realtor.com. The service I use to generate leads is called Commissions, Inc. (www.CommissionsInc.com). I like it because it provides me with a solid platform from which to drive traffic to our website. The key to any type of online service—because they are colder leads and people that you don't know—is getting on the phone and following up with these prospects within the first five or ten minutes of them hitting your website. If you don't do this quick follow-up, they will be off to the next real estate agent. In order to have a high conversion rate, you must have good systems in place for that follow-up. I've developed an effective follow up system called 3/4/12. My agents and coaching members often asked me how many times should they try to contact a lead before deleting it. I tell them that 80 percent of the leads are down-the-road leads, and we often don't convert those leads because we are trying to contact them too early in the process. The 3/4/12 system ensures you will never drop the lead too early and will have a higher conversion rate by following this system. Go to www.freewilliestuff.com to download a copy of my 3/4/12 follow-up plan.

Google Pay-Per-Click also generates a lot of traffic. Whether they're looking locally or they're looking across the country, often buyers will go to Google.com and just search "houses in Florida." With Google Pay-Per-Click, that's going to generate leads to your website if you pay for that traffic. Therefore, it's imperative to not only have an online presence but also to make sure that you have a working website when they get there.

You should also have personal and business Facebook pages. With those pages, you will be able to see what's going on in the lives of your clients, friends, and family based on their news feeds and what they're posting on Facebook. I can't tell you the number of times that I've been able to spot someone who's just had a baby, posting, "Here's another baby, and our house is going to be too small." Or I will see that someone's last child graduated from high school and is leaving home, and now the house feels too big. Using that information, I've been able to send them personal notes and messages, follow up with phone calls, and, in return, have them say, "Your timing on this note was great. We were just talking about selling."

You not only want to keep up with others' postings, but you also want to update your own Facebook page. People like to know what's going on in your life and hearing what's new with you and your family. They like to see testimonials from other happy clients that you post on your wall. For example, a posting that says, "Willie sold our house in 22 days at 98.6 percent of our asking price," is excellent advertising. I include a picture of a "Sold" sign in front of their home, and it works wonders. A Facebook photo of you in front of a buyer's new home handing them the keys is a picture that says a thousand words. Millennial buyers are all on Facebook. They're also on Twitter, LinkedIn, and Instagram. If you're going to service that segment of the market, then you have to be where that market is.

You must also have a website—an *easy, user-friendly* website. My website (www.WillieMiranda.com) provides both buyers and sellers with a great deal of information and offers reports that they can instantly download. It requires them to fill out their name, email address, and phone number, and once they complete that form and hit submit, it will generate reports to them, such as the "Top 5 Strategies to Sell Your Capital District Home Fast for Top Dollar with the Least Amount of Hassle," "6 Biggest Buyer Mistakes That Buyers Make When Buying a Home," or "27 Tips That All Sellers Need to Know to Sell Their Home Fast and For Top Dollar." People are always out there looking, doing searches on Google, being driven to your website; so it's vital that you give them good, valuable, solid information once they get there.

Videos can also be very effective on your website. Videos will drive your search engine optimization traffic much higher because people look at videos longer than they look at general text. I have a 30-minute infomercial on my website that describes my marketing. I also post customer video testimonials on the site because while I can say whatever I want to, people still believe third-party testimonials more than they believe what an agent says on a website. Videos show your body language and your personality. Let's face it, people are interviewing you online, and while they can't really interview you based on text, they definitely can based on a video. You can also upload your videos to YouTube and share them on multiple social media platforms to generate traffic back into your business. Check out some of my YouTube videos by going to YouTube.com and typing in "Willie Miranda Real Estate." Let me know what you think. Again, people do business with people they know, like, and trust, and you want to show them your competence as an agent, that you're knowledgeable, professional, and, most importantly, successful. Videos can do that for you.

OFFLINE
MARKETING

Don't neglect offline marketing. Not every buyer or seller out there is comfortable using a computer. I believe that the leads I get from our offline marketing strategies are more qualified because people are not hiding behind a computer. They're actually reaching out to us. They have to take the classified ad out of a newspaper and call an 800 number or email us directly. The ones who do contact us tend to be ready to go, because no one else is reaching out to that segment of the market. Traditional offline marketing can include classified ads, editorial ads, and postcards. If you send out postcards, make them worthwhile for both you and the customer. So many agents I see send out postcards, but there's no call to action implied if the card just reads, "Call Me, I'm #1." People don't care about that. People want to know what information they will get when they do call you. So offer them something. Give them a *reason* to call you.

To this day my favorite offline marketing tactic is the newsletter. If I had to give up all my offline marketing, the last one I would give up would be my newsletter. This four-page bulletin contains information about myself and what's going on in the clients' neighborhood. It gives them information on what has sold in the past six to twelve months and what properties are still pending or ready to close.

By sending this newsletter out to our clients, we provide them with information on what's going on around them and the approximate value of what their home is worth in today's market. (Download an example of my newsletter at www.freewilliestuff.com).

I have been sending newsletters out to targeted neighborhoods consistently over the last few years. I recently met with one family who was about to relocate. Sitting at the kitchen table with them, I proceeded to go into my listing presentation. About two or three slides in, the wife turned to me and said, "Willie, you can close that. You don't need to go through all of this. We're going to go with you." And I quickly and wisely shut off my computer. When people say things like that, you don't want to keep going with your presentation and then have them change their mind.

Then I said, "I know it's required by your relocation company that you meet with three agents. I'm wondering what made you know you wanted to go with me so quickly." She answered, "We met with the other two agents already and one we definitely know we're not going to use. She was very abrupt and brushed us off. The second agent we met was pretty good, but we feel like we already know you." I asked how that had happened. She responded, "We get your newsletter every month and a few months ago, when you and your family went to Paris, your newsletter had a picture of all of you in front of the Eiffel Tower. We have the same picture from our trip to Paris with our family!" It was at that point that I thought to myself this newsletter really does work because, again, people do business with people they know, like, and trust. They felt they already knew me. They felt they knew my family. They knew I coached my daughter Julia's softball team. They read my wife's recipes every month—recipes that have been handed down from generation to generation and are my family's favorites. This couple felt a connection to me.

I'm not alone in my affection for newsletters. Marketing guru Dan Kennedy says newsletters are one of the best marketing tools you can use in your business. Not an online marketing newsletter, which you send via email, because the open rates for online newsletters are maybe 15–20 percent at best. You want to send actual snail mail—a paper newsletter that you send out and that is delivered right to their mailbox. Kennedy adds that 60 percent of your newsletter should be non relevant to the real estate business, but rather about personal things going on in your life, even personal things that are happening with your team and staff. Every time we have an event going on at the office, we'll put those pictures in the newsletter. Whenever we have a staff member who has celebrated a birthday or had a new baby, that photo goes in there. People want to be connected. A newsletter makes your customers feel like they are part of your community or, in my case, the Willie Miranda Real Estate Community.

We also have personal brochures that we mail out. (A sample brochure is available for download at www.freewilliestuff.com).

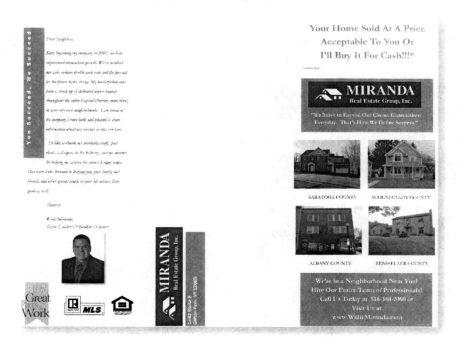

It is important for people to see what you are about, so give them information about yourself. In the real estate business, we pretty much wake up every day unemployed. As 1099 contractors, we're interviewing every day looking for that next job. If you don't have a real estate brochure, it's like not having a resume when looking for a job. A personal brochure is your resume for buyers and sellers moving forward and an important offline marketing tool to set you apart from your competition.

GEOGRAPHIC FARMING

You also need to appreciate the value of geographic farming. The goal is to build a real estate business that continually renews itself with repeat business. Geographic farming is one of the best ways to do that. In coaching and training agents over the years, I've encouraged them to market within a one or two-mile radius of their home, making sure that they do some type of monthly mailing to that geographic farm. I call it the "12 Direct," which is essentially mailing something out each and every month to that list.

In June 2013, I was taking a walk with my wife around our neighborhood. I saw a lot of "For Sale" signs up, but unfortunately, none of them were mine. I turned to my wife and said, "You know, I really need to start mailing something out to this neighborhood, a postcard or a newsletter." And I remember her stopping and saying, "Well, why don't you do it? You've been saying this now for the last couple of years and you haven't done it yet. You tell all your coaching members and agents to do it, but you haven't done it. You should probably practice what you preach." She was right. So I went ahead and put out both postcards and newsletters around my own neighborhood.

This actually took the form of a campaign. If I listed someone's house, I would send out a "Just Listed" postcard. Once it sold, I would send out a "Just Sold" card saying, "I just sold this house in 20 days at 95 percent of its asking price. If you're looking to get your home sold, give me a call." (You can download both of these postcards at www.freewilliestuff.com).

I ended up dominating that neighborhood. I had spent $7,000 in marketing for that neighborhood, and by the end of the first year with that campaign I had closed nine transactions, which generated more than $120,000 in commissions.

This can be done in any neighborhood. It's just a matter of being consistent, getting the right message out there, using testimonials for third-party endorsements, and employing the four-page newsletter to really deepen a relationship with that list, because eventually, it's all timing. Sooner or later people will move or know of other people who are planning to move, and they're going to call you with a referral. Thus, geographic farming becomes another valuable marketing tool.

Business-to-business (B2B) marketing is also effective. There are close to 35 different professions that are involved in any one real estate transaction. I have an online and an offline directory of recommended vendors that I distribute to our customers, such as carpet cleaners, attorneys, or mortgage people. When they're relocating from out-of-town and don't know anyone, I'm able to hand them this list and say, "Here are people that I can put my name to. Here are people that have done great work for other clients of mine." My clients appreciate it because it's another service I've provided, but it also helps my business vendors, many of whom do 100 percent of their business by referral. They don't pay me a fee for being on that list. I just ask that they give my customers good service. In turn, they have provided me with many referrals. Over the last 18 months, I've received five sales and listing appointments from my carpet cleaner, who is often in homes before they are put on the market. I've probably given him 20 different cleaning jobs over the years, so it becomes a win/win situation for all involved.

Lead generation is the pillar to success of any real estate business, and agents must have a systematic way of generating leads. Without leads, you have no business. If you only have one source of lead generation, then you're not going to be all that successful. At a minimum, I recommend the four pillars that I just talked about, and agents who have consistently used those four pillars have been successful in growing a consistent income-generating real estate business.

CHAPTER 2

· ·

DATABASE GOLD MINE:
THE FOUNDATION
OF SUCCESS

In 1991, fresh out of college, I was working for Prudential Financial Services selling life insurance. There was a gentleman there who turned out to be a significant mentor to me. His name was Sam Sterns. Sam was one of the top agents in the company, and I was amazed by how busy he was. He was an older man, but everyone knew and loved him, including his clients. He had business pouring in left and right. So I asked him if I could take him to lunch and pick his brain. When I met with Sam, my first question was, "What are the top three things I need to do to be successful?" He said, "The first thing you need to do is *not* be in the office. There's no one in this office you can sell insurance to. I would recommend you start going door-to-door." So he taught me how to go door-to-door and what to say. He showed me how to work an auto dealership. The dealership sales representatives were always in front of people with new cars, and by working with dealerships, I was able to get into the auto and homeowner insurance business.

So Sam's first two tips were (1) don't be in the office and (2) start generating auto and homeowner policies through dealerships. His third tip? Start building your database. The best advice he gave me was something I'll never forget. Sam told me that the success or failure of your business is in direct proportion to the number of people in your database. This stuck with me, because Sam's database was huge. At that time anyone who was new to the business received a metal card file box with a few hundred client records to use. They called those cards OPSR cards, or orphan service records. Sam had a lot of cards, and he would go through and call everyone in his database. He knew them all, knew their kids, and knew everything about their family insurance needs. Some of the people he had had as customers for 35–40 years. Early on, Sam showed me the importance and value of a well-managed database.

The other thing Sam taught me about was referrals. When he was face-to-face with clients, he would get referrals from their family and friends because he would *ask* for them. He would literally ask, "Who else can we help?" The clients would feel compelled to give him the information because they wanted their own family and friends to benefit from and have the same type of financial security that Sam was able to provide them.

Sam would also ask his clients a lot of key questions about their family. He would find out if there were births, if anyone had just bought a new home, or perhaps if anyone was downsizing because of children going off to college. He would also talk about their retirement plans. Eighty to 100 percent of the business Sam did came from repeat and referral business.

From Sam, I learned at a young age how a successful agent was able to build a profitable business. That card system had to be lugged around in the trunk of our cars, because we didn't have computers back then. It was the only database we had to use. As the saying goes, we've come a long way, baby.

Later, I took all those tips that I had learned from Sam in the insurance business and applied them to my real estate business as well. I eventually converted my one-card database system to a software computer program called ACT. A few years later, I changed to a more real estate-based software program called Agent Office. That worked well for me for almost a decade, and today I use a software program called Top Producer. I like this database because it is compatible with social media and has a number of Internet capabilities. It also interfaces well with smartphones.

I am still astounded that with all the technology available today, most agents don't have a database. Even agents who have been in the business 20–30 years don't reach out to their clients on a regular basis. Those are the agents I referred to before as transactional agents. Transactional agents are happy to just get by, but they could be a heck of a lot more successful if they had a systematic database. The average transactional agent sells about seven homes a year. The problem is they leave a lot of money on the table and have no client loyalty. They just assume that clients are going to call them when they're ready to buy, and that's not true at all. You need to be intentional and reach out to your clients on a consistent basis in order for them to think of you at the time of buying or selling a home.

Any time I coach agents, I push them toward the career agent path. I help them understand the importance of having a powerful systematic database where they can stay top of mind with their best prospects and clients. On average, a career agent sells between 24 to 36 homes a year. Over the years, I have found career agents to be more successful because they recognize the importance of the goldmine that is in their database. At the end of the day, the entire value of your business is in your database relationships.

In my coaching I use an easy three-step process to put agents on track.

STEP 1:

The first step, as I mentioned in chapter 1, is to gather all the names of their family, friends, past customers, and new customers—ultimately everyone they know or have done or would do business with in the future. Once they have all those names together, I encourage them to enter the contacts into a software program such as Top Producer and then sort them into five different categories.

1. The top category, which I call the VIP category, consists of your biggest raving fans. These are people who have given you multiple referrals in the past or have sold or bought several homes from you. As soon as the topic of real estate comes up in conversation, they are giving your cards out and they are referring your name.

2. The next category consists of your A clients. These are clients you have done business with in the past or people who have given you referrals before.

3. Then you have your B clients. This category includes people you have had conversations with about giving you referrals. You may not have done business with them or you may not have received a referral from them yet, but they have indicated that if they knew of anyone looking to buy or sell, they would definitely recommend you.

4. The subsequent category comprises your C clients. These are pretty much catch-all prospects. These are going to be Internet leads, people you met at an open house, people you interacted with at a networking event, or just people that you've met out and about. They know who you are, you know who they are, but you really haven't had a discussion yet of whether or not they would use or recommend you as an agent.

5. The last category contains your D clients. These are the people you don't want to do business with but who you keep in your database for reporting purposes. They are in there so you can track a transaction you did with them or because they came to your website for a certain report. You want to categorize them separately, but you don't want to be wasting marketing dollars on them. The goal, of course, is to move people from C to B, from B to A, and from A to VIP.

After you have gathered all the names and categorized them, what you do next is very important. You want to send them a simple one-page referral introduction letter. Or if they are not new to your business, you want to send them a letter to remind them again of what you do, who you work for, and to *ask* if they know of anyone looking to buy or sell. Let them know you're there to help and that you want to grow your business through referrals. Throw in a business card and your personal brochure. That's step number one: getting all of the information, categorizing it, and sending that letter out.

STEP 2:

· ·

The mistake a lot of agents make is that they send the referral letter out and think their phone is going to ring off the hook. The reality is that it doesn't happen that way. People will stick the cards in the drawer or they'll keep it in the back of their mind, but they may not have a need or know anyone looking to buy or sell real estate for several months. It's up to you to stay fresh in their minds so they don't forget who you are and will remember how to get a hold of you. I recommend doing that with the four-page newsletter we discussed in chapter 1.

You can create the newsletter yourself, or you can use a company to do it for you. I started with ServiceForLife.com, a real estate-related newsletter company that services real estate agents. They have a good template, but it doesn't have a lot of personal information in it. I recommend you include pictures and personal recipes in there, as you want to have fun stuff as well as real estate information. Today, I use Newsletter Pro. They have excellent graphic arts, and they call me every month to interview me and design the newsletter around that. They'll also print it and mail it for me.

Staying top of mind like this is vital, and in Step 2, I encourage making 29 touches out to your VIP, A, and B clients throughout the year. Some of the ways to do that is with "Just Listed" and "Just Sold" postcards, quarterly market updates, birthday cards or video emails, personal phone calls, and/or anniversary cards. You will make 12 of those 29 touches alone with your monthly newsletter. Everything else can be made up through the other sources I just mentioned.

STEP 3:

The third and last step is probably the most important because, as I've said, the money is in the follow-up. You must pick up the phone. You must call your client database, just like agents did back in the day. Those Prudential agents like Sam were successful because they picked up the phone, went to that client's home, or went door-to-door so that they were face-to-face with people. Most agents push this step to the side until it just never gets done. When I ask them why, they say they don't know what to say, or they don't feel comfortable showing up to the door or picking up the phone and calling.

In Step 3, I call and offer each and every one of our clients an annual home value report. That annual home value report is important because, for most clients, their biggest asset is really their home and no one else is calling them every year to give them an evaluation of their home. I want to make sure, just like their financial adviser gives them information on their 401(k) retirement plan, that as a real estate professional I am giving them information on what is selling around them and for what price, so they can get a ballpark idea of what their home is currently worth in today's market.

We prepare a CMA summary, which gives clients a Cost Market Analysis of the active, pending, and sold homes in the last 12 months in their area.

Since agents have already reported feeling uncomfortable on the phone, I have developed a sample script for this call. (Download the script at www.freewilliestuff.com.) Essentially, we call them to let them know that part of our service is to provide them with this annual home value report to give them an idea of the value their home is worth on the market today. I ask them if they would be interested in receiving it, and I have to say 99 percent of the people I ask do want a copy of the report.

The reason I call first is because I want to explain to them that it is just an estimate, a ballpark figure of what homes are selling for in the area. Otherwise, they just receive an actual amount in the mail; they can get concerned and confused because it could be off $50,000 in any one direction. We want to make sure we explain to them that they will be receiving only an *estimate* and that once they receive and review it, they need to follow up and call us to review it with them in more detail.

The CMA (Cost Market Analysis) expands your relationship with that client and it gives you an excuse to call them. It is a good strategy, and with the script template, it is easy to use, especially for those agents who have call reluctance. In turn, the law of reciprocity kicks in here because you are giving your clients something of value every year, and at the end of your call, you can ask whom else they know who might be interested in receiving this report. Finally, I always end the call by asking if they know anyone looking to buy or sell a home. I let them know how much I appreciate their referrals.

ANNUAL HOME VALUE REPORT SCRIPT

Hi… May I speak to <CLIENT> please? Hi <CLIENT> this is Willie from Miranda Real Estate Group. How are you doing today?

<MARY>…I just wanted to give you a quick call because I know it's been <JUST OVER/ALMOST> < # > years since you bought your home with me and from time to time I like to provide my clients with a free Annual Home Value Update. This update will give you a ball park idea of what your home is currently worth in today's market based on what other homes are selling for in your area.

So, I'm calling you today to see if you would be interested in receiving this free home value report?

Yes…99% of the time

Okay great, what is the best email address for me to send this report to? <If no email, send by regular mail>

So <CLIENT>, as I mentioned, this report is only a ballpark figure based on what other homes have sold for in your area. Please review the report and let me know if you have any questions.

One last thing <CLIENT>, do you know of anyone else who would also be interested in receiving this report for their home?

I'll get this information right out to you.

Now…If you know of anyone looking to buy or sell a home, please give me a call with their name and number and I will take good care of them. (Willie Bucks optional)

I recommend that every agent spend a minimum of two hours a day making these phone calls and doing their prospect follow-ups, whether it be through Internet leads, client follow-ups, sending personal notes, or putting reports together. Two hours a day minimum. The 80/20 rule applies here. If you just use two hours a day, five days a week, that is ten hours a week—which is 20 percent of your workweek, assuming a 50-hour work week. That 20 percent of pro-activity represents 80 percent of your results. The agents who spend two hours a day prospecting—doing these pro-activities, reaching out to their client base, sending them personal notes, going door-to-door, doing client visits—these are the ones who are doing 24 to 36 sales a year on average and making well over $100,000 a year because of the 80/20 rule.

The last thing I want to talk about in this chapter is the Client Close Plan (also available on www.freewilliestuff.com). The Client Close Plan works like this: the very first day after closing, I call the customer to see how things went at the closing, how things are going in their new home, and if they need any assistance from me at all to make sure they are happy with my services. I then send them a personal note in the mail repeating the same sentiments.

On day seven, I reach out to them again. It's been a week now, and I ask if there are any vendors that I can recommend. Perhaps they need a painter, a roofer, or a carpenter? I send them to our website to let them know that we have a client vendor directory posted there.

Thirty days after closing, I do a quick check-in call with the buyers to see how things are going. Then each and every year at day 365, I do an annual home value call with them. So I'm staying in touch with my client before, during, and after the sale. I have had some wonderful experiences deepening the relationship and going above and beyond giving that client excellent service through this kind of follow-up.

For instance, in one case, I called the client the day after the closing. He mentioned that he was a little upset because the prior sellers didn't leave their house keys as they were supposed to. He added that his wife was distressed because she felt there were keys out there for her home; they were in someone else's hands, and she didn't feel safe in her new home. So I called my locksmith that day and had him go over to the house that afternoon and re-key the whole house for them. It only cost me about $175 to do this, but the buyer was very impressed that I handled the situation for him. Within the next few months, I had received three more referrals from that client, and each referral mentioned how happy my client was with my services and the locksmith story he had shared with them.

Because I had a Client Close Plan, I was able to take care of this family and give them exceptional service. In turn, that close follow-up plan generated about $1.5 million more in business for me that year as a result of those three referrals. So again, the money is in the follow-up. But you have to have a systematic way of doing the follow-up in order to receive referrals in the future.

In closing, a database should make your prospects feel part of your community and deepen your relationships. I can't say it enough: people want to do business with someone they know they can trust. You want to make sure you develop your relationships with your customers so that they will go out of their way to help you secure more referral business in the future.

CHAPTER 3

· ·

B2B NETWORKING:
THE ALLIANCES OF SUCCESS

A lead-generation pillar that I see overlooked by many real estate agents across the country is the B2B (business-to-business) networking pillar. This is one of my favorite pillars, because I am able to relate to so many of the business owners in my community. We are all looking for new business. And we all rely heavily on repeat and referral business in order to keep our businesses going. Other business owners understand the importance of referrals. So when I ask business owners if they know of anyone looking to buy or sell a home, it is an easier conversation to start, and they are good sources of referrals.

Looking back over the years, I can see that the average sales price I have received from my business partners is much higher than the average sales price in our market. The reason for this is that business owners tend to know other professional business owners, which leads to a much higher sales price and sales volume.

The other reason that the referral from a business owner is a better referral is due to the relationship that the business owner has with that client. In other words, people do business with whom they know, like, and trust; therefore, if the client has a good business relationship with that business owner, when that business owner refers my name to the client, it carries a lot more weight. These clients are coming to me with total trust from the referral source (the business owner), and they tend to be a much easier client to work with versus a client off a cold call or from the Internet.

In order to take advantage of the B2B relationships you have, first you must build a business directory. Gather all the business relationships you are currently working with or have worked with in the past, starting with the professions that are most related to real estate. These might be roofers, mortgage lenders, attorneys, home appraisers, pest inspectors—the list goes on and on. As I said, there are more than 35 different professions that are directly related to any one real estate transaction.

Once you have an actual list, create an Excel sheet where you put the business vendor titles on one side, and then put their name, address, and phone number on the other side of the spreadsheet. Start with the names of people that you know. After that, reach out to your own client base. It is a great conversation to be able to pick up the phone and call your own clients to ask them whom they recommend. Let them know that you are building a business directory and that you are looking for a reputable name for a moving company or whatever business is lacking from your list. Make sure they know you will be using the directory to help future clients with their business referral needs. Many times, your own customers will give you excellent recommendations.

In my database, I have included many other professions that are not as closely related to real estate, such as a florist or massage therapist. I also have chiropractic groups, because if you just moved an entire house, you might be in need of a chiropractor.

I want my business clients to know that I am trying to refer business to them. In turn, I hope they will refer business to me. I have close to 75 different vendors in my business directory. I don't recommend just one to a client; I always mention two or three different mortgage lenders or attorneys whom the client can call and choose from. The first step is taking the time to compile that business vendor list.

Once you have that list created, then you can either prepare a Word document or put together a business directory that you can distribute to your clients. I like to hand out our business directory on an annual basis. I update it every year and provide it in a booklet form as well as make it available on our website for easy customer access. It provides them with everything they need to complete their move into a new community successfully. Years after the sale has been completed, I still find many of my clients calling me directly for referrals. That's because I have become the hub for my clients, and they trust that I will send them a quality vendor that will do a great job for them. This is why it is important to build that alliance with each of your business vendors. You want to make sure that you're the first name that comes to mind when a real estate need arises.

Once you establish the directory, you must let those relationships know exactly what you do in your profession and what constitutes a good referral for you. The best way to do that is to meet face to face with these people. It requires a little bit of work, but the benefits are definitely worth the time that you take to build an alliance with these vendors.

Call each of them and offer to meet with them at their place of work. I prefer going to their establishment because it allows me to see behind the scenes of their business. It gives me a good indication as to whether or not I will want to refer my clients to those vendors.

Your goal should be to find out what a good referral is for them too, as I have never found a business professional who didn't want to receive referrals. They have a good idea of what the sweet spots are in their business and what a good client is for them. After you establish that and talk to them about what their goals with the business are in the next three to five years, only then should you discuss your business with them.

Give them some background on your real estate business: how you got started and how you have grown. If they are good business people, which most are, they have experience with repeat and referral business percentages. In other words, once they have built up their clientele, they will notice a significant decrease in their marketing budgets as a direct result of receiving more referral business. They want your referrals, and we want referrals from them.

In closing, ask them for permission to add them to your business directory. I don't ask for any money from them, but I do ask if there is any type of discount they can pass on to my clients. It might be just a flat dollar amount off a certain service, such as a coupon for up to $200 off their closing costs, or it could be a percentage—say 20 percent off on their next power washing. Thus, the directory becomes similar to a concierge service for your clients, and it provides a tremendous value to them.

Also offer some type of cross-promotion for the vendor's clients. For example, if they have a newsletter that they send out, ask if you can put in some type of offer for their clients (I offer a "$500 Willie Bucks" certificate to use during their closing). The vendor, when mailing out the newsletter, might include an endorsement letter that provides information about your business and lets their clients know they have had good experiences working with you. What better way to get a referral than from one of your business partners reaching out to their happy customers? It makes for a really good exchange and value for everyone involved.

I'll do the same thing with my monthly newsletter, where I will spotlight a business vendor in a half-page section. I'll add a photo of my business owner and talk about the benefits of using their services, mentioning how they have done a great job for me. This creates a win/win situation for both the business vendor and me.

Another way for real estate agents to network is to attend Chamber of Commerce events or belong to various leadership groups, such as Business Networking International (BNI). But don't just show up, put your name tag on, shake hands, listen to a presentation, hand out and receive a couple of business cards, and then go home and stick them in your top desk drawer. When you go to those mixers, start with a goal of collecting a minimum of five business cards. When you get home, don't just put the cards away in your desk or bureau drawer. Take the time to look through them for vendors that you might need to fill the gaps in your business directory or that may be a good referral source to exchange clients with.

Once again, the follow-up is key. The next morning, send out a personal note with your business card to let them know you enjoyed meeting them, and ask to get together with them over coffee to learn a little more about their business. Along with your business card, include your personal brochure that will give them some background on your services as well.

I recommend following up again three to five business days later to see if they received your card and to set up a time to meet. Remember, you are not trying to sell them but rather to connect regarding an exchange of referrals. In my experience, I have found most business vendors are more than happy to meet for a short period of time. At the meeting, show them your business directory, and tell them how it works. Reinforce that there's no fee for being listed in the directory, but they do need to deliver exceptional service when called upon from our clients. Let them know they can expect the same exceptional service to anyone they refer to you. Leave the meeting on a positive tone.

After that encounter, send them a personal note thanking them for meeting with you. Include some of your business cards, and ask them to mail you their business cards if you don't already have them. Add them to your directory and monthly newsletter. The monthly newsletter is the glue that keeps your name in front of them so that when the conversation of real estate comes up, you are the first name that comes to their mind. This has been far more effective and resulted in more referrals from business partners than sticking their business cards in my top desk drawer.

Another way to deepen your relationships with your business network is by hosting a business mixer for your vendors. This can turn out to be your most profitable lead-generation pillar if done correctly.

The purpose behind the business vendor mixer is to meet and exchange business cards. But the other message you want to send is that it is a privilege, not a right, to be a part of this event. In other words, they have to give your clients exceptional service in order to stay on that invite list year after year.

Prepare for the mixer four to five weeks prior to the event date. Make reservations at the establishment (you can hold it at a country club, golf club, restaurant, or store) and choose the menu. Have your lender pay or share expenses for the hors d'oeuvres and any food related to the mixer. Set up a cash bar from 5 to 7 p.m. This not only helps keep the expenses down but also keeps the liability down as well.

Then compose an agenda and generate your guest list. Reach out to the business owners in your directory and invite them to the actual mixer. First, send them a "Save The Date" email, and then follow up with a phone call to make sure they received it. Finally, send them a postcard invitation as well. Ask them to bring another business owner with them that they have a good relationship with who is not in your directory and who does exceptional work. They might bring someone who could be added to your business directory and be a huge referral source to you in the future.

A couple of days before the mixer, make phone calls to those who RSVP'd to remind them to bring their business cards. Because it is a networking event, look at the RSVP list and see who is coming so you can match people up at the event. In this way, they will get more leverage that will complement their business.

On the day of the actual mixer, arrive early. You want to be there to greet your guests as they arrive. Check them off the guest list as they come in, and give them their nametags. Collect their business cards so you can update their current information, and then add the cards to the raffle bowl.

You also want to make sure that you establish the date for the next mixer so that you can announce it that evening. Keep it around the same time of the year. I have found that fall (September or October) works best, usually on a Wednesday or Thursday evening after most get off work.

At the event, once everyone has signed in, play a "break the ice" type of game, such as giving each guest ten questions they must answer (i.e., find out who went to a certain university or who has a birthday that month). Then have people go around the room asking these questions. This will help to get everyone talking to each other and getting to know others they can do business with in the future.

After that, make an opening introduction, thanking everyone for coming and reinforcing why they are there: they are doing a great job, they are part of your referral directory. Let them know you appreciate them going the extra mile for your customers, and assure them that you will go above and beyond for their clients, as well. Keep it brief, five to ten minutes at most, and then have your lender speak, as he or she is sponsoring the event with you. Again, just a quick five minutes to talk about the bank and mention what the bank can do for these business vendors on a commercial level. The rest of the event consists of everyone networking with each other and passing out business cards for about an hour and a half to two hours.

The day after the mixer, it is important to make phone calls and thank those who attended the event, asking them for their feedback. This is also a chance to set up one-on-one meetings with vendors you haven't met to learn more about their businesses. Then send out a personal note to thank everyone who attended, and include any photos you may have taken of them at the event.

Never underestimate the value and power of working your B2B relationships. All of us have tremendous resources within our own databases to put together a very strong and powerful referral network of business vendors. It doesn't take long to do it, and it is simple to do. It is just a matter of making your business directory feel like a club or business community that they belong to: i.e., the Miranda Real Estate Business Directory.

CHAPTER 4

. . . .

TIME MANAGEMENT:
THE KEY TO SUCCESS

One of the biggest challenges real estate agents face each day is getting everything done that we set out to do and keeping everyone around us happy. This task doesn't have to be as challenging as it seems, or as some of us allow it to be.

By taking control and having the right systems in place, you can manage and protect your time just like you manage the rest of your business. All it takes is adding discipline and routine to what you do each day. When you are planning your days and weeks, remember to keep in mind the things that are important, not only in business but also with your family. By maintaining one calendar for everything you do, you can efficiently plan your business, family, and personal social activities. Be sure to schedule items in your calendar that are most essential to you first, and then work around them.

Time management is the difference between top-performing people and those who constantly struggle. We all have the same number of hours every day, but why is it that some real estate agents do well over a $1 million in commission every year, and other agents who work just as hard, if not harder, barely make $50,000 a year in commissions?

The difference between the two is time management. Successful agents manage their time better and focus on the activities (or pro-activities) that will generate the highest return for their business.

We all fool ourselves by saying we work 12-hour days. When you really analyze what your productivity is throughout the day, you'd be shocked at how much time you waste on doing nothing. And things that are not pro-active do not add value to your business. As real estate agents, we get paid the most money by prospecting, listing homes, selling homes to buyers, and negotiating. Everything else should be delegated to an assistant.

Craig Proctor taught me a time management tool to use to evaluate a daily schedule. For one week, at every half-hour, jot down what you did in that half-hour block. You will be shocked at all the time you squandered doing things that were not proactive. Whether it was hanging out by the water cooler or going to lunch for a couple hours with another agent, you'll find yourself jotting down a lot of time wasted on non-income-producing activities.

In his book *The Ultimate Sales Machine*, Chet Holmes outlines six steps to organize your schedule so that you can focus on the right things, things that are proactive for your business. They are:

The Ultimate Sales Machine on Time Management

1. Touch it Once

2. Make Lists

3. Plan how much time you will allocate to each task

4. Plan the Day

5. Prioritize

6. Ask Yourself, "Will it hurt me to throw this away"

STEP 1. TOUCH IT ONCE.

As real estate agents, our paperwork becomes tremendous. We could spend tons of time on paperwork, and handling it inefficiently is a huge waste of time, especially if you are handling it more than once without a system for completing it.

An example of a system to help you only touch it once is utilizing a software program such as Evernote. Evernote allows you to clip web articles, capture handwritten notes, and snap photos so you can keep digital details of your projects. You can scan or take pictures of things you want to keep for future reference. You can forward emails to your Evernote account. All of it is stored in one central location in the cloud. Anytime you need something, you can reference it by typing in a name or word from the document you want to recall, and Evernote will pull it right up for you. It will allow you to become almost paperless in your office. Think about all the time you waste looking through files and paperwork on your desk that should be filed and never looked at again until needed.

STEP 2. MAKE LISTS.

Lists are very important. We all tend to write things on paper napkins, sticky notes, or the backs of business cards. This is an easy way to lose leads and phone numbers. Learn to put everything down on a sheet of yellow lined paper. Go through and list everything that is on your mind or anything that needs to be done. It doesn't mean that it is going to get done that second, but it is on the list so you won't forget about it.

If a client asks you to get back to him on a cost market analysis or says she would like you to list her home Saturday morning at 10:00, and all you do is jot it on a sticky note, you might misplace that small piece of paper. That slip-up could cost you thousands of dollars in commissions in a lost sale. But if it is on your yellow pad list, you are far less likely to lose track of it.

As real estate agents, we get paid the most amount of money by prospecting, listing homes, selling homes to buyers, and negotiating. Everything else should be delegated to an assistant.

STEP 3. PLAN HOW MUCH TIME YOU WILL ALLOCATE TO EACH TASK.

When you plan your day, be realistic. You can only get to five or six major items on that list. So if your list runs seven to ten sheets of paper, create a separate list for each day. Now, go through that to-do list and circle the things that you feel are an A-plus priority, items that must get done that day or within the next 24 hours. Pull those off, and put them on a separate list.

Allocate your time. If you pull five or six different to-dos off your master list, the only way they are going to get done is if you time-block them into your schedule. If you don't have each item blocked in your schedule, other things will pop up and manage your time for you.

So, if you need to prepare for a home listing the next day, and you need to do some research or a cost market analysis and marketing plan, block out one hour the day before to do that research and create a good presentation for that seller. Write it into your schedule just like an appointment and shut off all the phones and other distractions, because phones and emails are time vampires.

Time vampires are the constant interruptions that you receive during the day in an office. Whether it is people walking up to your desk or coworkers giving you the old "got a minute?", we all know that one minute quickly turns into 15 to 30 minutes. Anything that controls our time for us is a time vampire. That is why you should list and then allocate adequate time for important tasks that you need to accomplish in your schedule.

STEP 4. PLAN YOUR DAY.

On Sunday nights, my wife and I look at our schedules together and plan out the next two weeks. It doesn't take more than 15-20 minutes to do, but it is vitally important.

The reason I am attracted to the real estate business in the first place is the time flexibility. The reason I see other agents fail in this business is because they don't know how to use that flexibility to their advantage. They were told what to do and when to do it in their prior jobs. As real estate agents, we are entrepreneurs, and as entrepreneurs we have to be very disciplined to control that flexibility. Not controlling your time on the right activities will take you out of this business quickly, because you will not make the sales you need to survive in this business.

STEP 5. PRIORITIZE.

Every real estate agent's top priority must be prospecting and doing pro-activities that are going to generate sales for their business.

You have heard it over and over again: 20 percent of your efforts will bring in 80 percent of your results. It is very important that you don't get stuck doing busy work, because busy work is part of the 80 percent that won't make you money. The 20 percent includes the pro-activities that are going to give you 80 percent of your sales results. Set aside a two-hour time frame in your schedule *every day* to make between 40 and 50 calls. In reality, you are probably only going to reach a third of the people you call. Whether it is calling your past clients, calling your current clients, or calling on leads from the website, you want to make sure that you block out two hours a day for that dollar-productive activity.

By not scheduling these priorities, you will find yourself being more reactive than proactive. You want to be in a proactive position rather than a reactive position, and that is where you will find yourself if you have your day planned out ahead of time. If you just show up at the office and just go with the flow, then you are letting everyone else dictate your day.

STEP 6. ASK YOURSELF, "WILL IT HURT ME TO THROW THIS AWAY?"

Eighty percent of all the paper we file away never gets referred to again. Make good use of scanning your files and storing the files on your server or using a program like Evernote to store online. You can locate the information more easily and waste a lot less time looking through messy and bulky filing cabinets.

Everyone wants to be their own boss—until they are. Being your own boss comes at a price, and that price is managing time correctly. If you don't use your time efficiently and on important tasks, in the end that is exactly what will put you out of business.

Come up with what works for you. I was able to apply time management tactics that I learned from Dan Kennedy and Chet Holmes books to my business. These tactics have worked well for me, but everyone is different. Some people like to have a paper format for their schedule. I like to put my schedule on my smartphone because I can share that calendar with my wife. She can then put in doctors' appointments, sporting events, and birthday dinners. Those are my big rocks—the things I don't want to miss. Then I work around those dates. If that means I work from 8–10 o'clock at night on a project because I needed to be home from 4–6 p.m. for a birthday party, then that is what I do. I am here to say that you can have a great family life *and* a great business life if you have effective time management skills and plan your schedule every day accordingly.

Here are my five time management must-dos:

5 Time Management Must Do's

1. **Plan your week.**
2. **Plan your day.**
3. **Control Incoming Calls.**
4. **Schedule 2 hours proactive (lead generation) activities a day.**
5. **Take at least one day off per week.**

1. PLAN YOUR WEEK.

By planning your week, you build structure into your life. The use of only one calendar is imperative to avoid losing track of appointments, since missing an appointment can cost you thousands of dollars.

You also want to schedule time off. Time off is not going to just appear on your schedule. You actually have to schedule it. I recommend taking at least one day off a week. If you can't do it on the weekend, then take a day off during the week to spend time with your family or do personal things you enjoy. You also want to carve out time for healthy activities. So if you need to get to the gym three or four days a week, block that into your schedule.

I have a schedule template that I call the "perfect week" that I give to agents. You can get a copy of it by going to www.freewilliestuff. com. I break it down from going to the gym four days a week to checking emails and voice mails three times a day to blocking pro-activity time, and at the end of each day, make time to plan your following day.

I mention only checking your emails and voice mails three times a day, because studies show that every time you stop to look at emails it takes you about 12 minutes to refocus on what you were doing. So shut the email alert ringer off on your computer, because there is nothing that urgent that should interfere with your pro-activities.

2. PLAN YOUR DAY.

Take 15 minutes the night before to plan the next day. First list out your follow-up calls. You want to get back to people in a timely manner. Don't wait two to three days to follow up with someone. Block those power calls into your two hours of proactivity time.

Next, add in your to-do items, and last is everything else. You want to prioritize in that direction. You don't leave the important calls and meetings to the end where they might get neglected, or worse, not done at all.

3. CONTROL INCOMING CALLS.

Incoming calls are huge time vampires and something that need to be controlled. That is why we have voice mail. But some people feel they have to answer every call for fear that they are going to miss a lead or a sale.

Last week I was doing a training class for 15 of my agents. We spent about two hours focusing on how to better grow our referral business. During this meeting, I noticed that one of my agents was a little fidgety. I asked her if everything was okay.

She said, "Everything's fine but I left my phone at home."

I said, "No problem. When the class is over, you're more than welcome to go home and get your phone. Are you sure everything will be okay?"

She said, "Yes, but I might get an offer on this one property and I don't want to miss the agent calling me."

I said, "You're not going to miss anything. Right now, you have blocked out your schedule for training, and this is more important in helping you grow your business. I'm sure that offer will still be good two hours from now."

Over the next half-hour, I noticed that she was still a little fidgety and not as focused as she needed to be. Then, all of a sudden at the break, she started packing up all her stuff, put her coat on, and she said, "Willie, I can't stand it. I've got to go home and get my phone. I'm sorry. I'll see you tomorrow."

It really comes down to the cell phone being an addiction, but it can also create a lot of stress and anxiety.

I view a cell phone as a huge problem because of all the distractions it creates. It doesn't allow you to disconnect from society and focus on the important things you need to do or be engaged with. The constant texting and social media distractions are becoming the biggest time vampires in our business, and those who learn how to disconnect from them will be the most productive and successful.

Many studies have already proven this to be true, and it will be interesting to see how most agents handle this problem in the future.

You can control incoming calls by leaving a message on your voice mail that says you will be doing just that. For example, I have a voice mail script that says, "Hi, you've reached Willie Miranda with Miranda Real Estate Group. Please note that I will be in meetings throughout the day and returning phone calls between 11 and 12, and again between 4 and 5 p.m. For immediate assistance, please contact my office at (XXX) 555-5555. Or leave your name and number after the tone, and I'll return your call as soon as possible. Thank you and have a great day."

By leaving that script on my voice mail, I'm showing callers that I'm in meetings or taking care of other clients. People appreciate it because they know you are going to give them a call back within a certain time frame. It is very important that you do follow-through on returning calls, because you will quickly lose credibility if you don't call back within the time frame you promised.

I use a tool called a voice mail log from Rediform. Every time you listen to a voice mail, write it down and put it on this format or on your to-do list. It is a great checklist for you to refer back to weeks or months from now. But more importantly, it keeps you from having to go back and listen to all of your voice mails again, wasting even more time.

The one thing that really irks me is when I call a real estate agent's phone and I get a message that says, "Sorry, this mailbox is full." There is no reason any agent should have a full voice mailbox if they are retrieving all of their messages and returning those phone calls in a timely manner.

Structure return calls by blocking your new leads, your seller calls, and buyer clients into the first segment of your calling. You could also write personal notes in this first two-hour block. I encourage my agents to write at least five personal notes a day to people they talked to that day or people they want to reach out to in the near future.

Another pro-activity is adding and deleting people in your database. A good database is only as good as the information you put in it. If you have people in your database that you know shouldn't be in there, remove them. Make sure to update your client information regularly and keep great notes on conversations you have with them. Clients are amazed at how much you remember about them and their families. Good notes will allow you to do this, and you will build a better bond with your clients.

A day without lead generation is a day that you didn't work. If you don't block off a minimum of two hours a day for lead generation, then you didn't work that day. I don't care how busy you were with closings or inspections or even sending out newsletters. I'll say it again, if you didn't block out at least two hours a day for lead generation, you simply didn't work that day. As I mentioned before, 20 percent of our effort returns 80 percent of our results. If you work 50 hours a week, 20 percent of that time is about ten hours a week. If you are working a five-day workweek, that's exactly two hours a day. Focus those two hours a day on proactivity, and that will bring in 80 percent of your sales results.

4. TAKE ONE DAY OFF PER WEEK.
· ·

I can't stress enough the importance of taking at least one day off to recharge and re-energize. If you can't take a full day, then definitely take at least two half-days off. If weekends are a challenge, take time off during the week. The body and mind require the time to rest and refocus.

5. CELEBRATE.

The other piece in planning your week is to schedule in celebrations. If you have a good month or quarter in sales, you definitely want to schedule in a celebration for that. For instance, I schedule in a massage appointment to celebrate goals I have achieved. Taking time for yourself will make you a much better real estate agent. Some may choose to buy a gift or take a day trip to a special place. It can be whatever you want it to be, but it is important to have something to look forward to as you accomplish the goals you set for yourself.

In closing, time management means you must prioritize, implement, and evaluate your schedule. Prioritize your A, B, C, and D list each and every day. Do your A's first. Be flexible about moving your B's and C's. Give yourself the grace that not everything will get done in one day. You can always push it to the following day.

Implement, implement, implement! Work hard and stay focused on getting your priorities done for that day and stick to your daily plan. Highly successful salespeople know how to implement and take action.

But at the end of each day, it is important to evaluate how well you managed your time. Before you go to bed, take a look at your list. There is something psychological about being able to cross things off your to-do list that will definitely have a positive impact on your business. You want to acknowledge those achievements with coworkers or family.

Determine what you could have done differently throughout the day and make future changes to improve them. Plan out your next day by creating a new to-do list. It's not good time management to keep running off the same list or sheet of paper.

To download a copy of my "Perfect Week Schedule" and to-do list visit: www.freewilliestuff.com.

CHAPTER 5

....

TEAM BUILDING: THE SUPPORTS OF SUCCESS

I picked up on the concept of team building many years ago when I worked at Prudential Financial Services. I learned from my mentor Sam Sterns, that time is money and that I shouldn't be focusing my time on low-dollar-cost activities, was an eye-opener to me. He continually stressed that I should delegate those tasks to other people so I could pay more attention on the higher-dollar-cost activities. Sam's mantra was, "That's how you make more money in the business. That's how you grow and become successful—by leveraging yourself with the right people."

Watching the way Sam and other top agents worked, I recognized the importance of having a team. But when I got into the real estate business, I noticed that most agents tried to do it all on their own:

create their own fact sheets, put up signs on lawns, put lock boxes on homes, take their own pictures, market their business, and work with buyers and sellers. The fact, is that you just can't do it *all*. I have found that once an agent sells about 25–30 homes in a year, they will start to notice a drop in sales and will reach a plateau. There just isn't enough time for them to get to it all, and this is when you need some help to get to the next level in your business.

You may feel you are the best person to do all those things, but in order to get to the next level of success, you need an assistant. Every time I've hired someone to help me with the overflow of work I had, I always saw an increase in my business production. I have always been able to justify bringing that person on board, as he or she brought multiple times their salary to the bottom line.

When I left RE/MAX in 2002 and went out on my own, I was working with a coach who advised me to hire someone to help me. There were a couple of times that I actually lost business because I wasn't able to get to a buyer quick enough. I was working with other buyers or sellers, and that buyer ended up calling someone else because they couldn't wait for me. There were times that I didn't call a listing lead back as soon as I should have because I was out on appointments, and I lost that business too. When you get to that point where you start losing business, then you know you need an assistant.

As I mentioned, my coach suggested taking the next two weeks and jotting down everything that I was doing in half-hour increments. If I got up at eight o'clock to check emails, I wrote that down. If I was going on a listing appointment, I wrote that down. If I was preparing for a listing appointment, I wrote that down. At the end of the two weeks, I met with my coach again and he had me circle everything on the list that I could easily delegate to someone else. I went through the entire record and found there were 25–30 different tasks that I could pay someone else to do, from writing up fact sheets to inputting data into the Multiple Listing Service to making copies to putting my signs up. There were so many things that I was wasting my time running around doing that I could pay someone else $10 or $15 an hour to do. I could be making $100 to $500 an hour if my time was focused on pro-activities, but instead I was spending my time doing $10–$15 an hour work that I could pay someone else to do.

Having analyzed those numbers, I immediately hired someone to work for me part-time. I had her shadow me and take notes so she could understand exactly what I did and how I did it. We did this for more than 25 tasks, and that's how we created the part-time assistant's job description.

That was the first stage of how I built my team. I started off the Miranda Real Estate Group with four people. My original goal was to have a small team. As time went on, I attracted more and more agents who wanted to work with our team. I began to have a lot of leads that I couldn't follow up on myself, so it was important for me to bring more people on board to take care of them.

Author Napoleon Hill wrote, "It is literally true that you can succeed best and quickest by helping others to succeed." I have always aimed to help the agents who come to work for me by building their business within my business. By helping them succeed, our company has become more successful over the years. As a result, I went from just myself, to a very small team, to a large team, and now to a large independent brokerage at Miranda Real Estate Group.

When I was building my team, I would start buyer agents at a 50 percent split. If I gave them a lead, they would get 50 percent of the commission. But as time went on and the margins became smaller in the real estate business, that model was just not profitable anymore. With the high cost of advertising and marketing and having a good team structure in place with sufficient administrative support, it's not feasible to pay agents 50 percent of the business that comes through for simply showing three or four houses. At that rate, I was paying them $500 to $1,000 per hour.

I knew there had to be a better way. At a conference, I met with some of the top teams around the country, and one of those teams used what they called a "showing agent." They also employed a "listing agent." Instead of having buyer agents who they paid leads out to at a 50 percent split, they hired showing agents. Showing agents still did their own business and built their own clientele, but they were willing to show properties for an hourly rate and receive a bonus once the home closed.

I hired a couple of showing agents. I would sit with my clients, sign them to the buyer contract, do my presentation, and then I'd say, "My showing assistant is going to make all arrangements to view your desired homes and accompany the showings. When you find the property you want to purchase, I'll come out and take a look to let you know what I think, and then I'll sit down and negotiate the contract for you. Negotiating is really where you want me because my expertise is getting you top dollar when selling your home or finding the right home for you at the lowest price when buying a home." Most buyers were comfortable knowing that I would be involved in the transaction when it came to that point, but they also realized that they didn't need me to go out and just open up doors for them. I also reinforced that my showing agents had a more flexible schedule than I did, so they would be able to get them into properties much more quickly than I could.

The showing agents like it because they get paid whether or not that client ever buys a home. I'm paying them $20–$25 per hour to go and show properties, and when that home closes, I'll also give them a $250 bonus. That's far less than the $500 to $1,000 an hour I was paying by doing a 50/50 split, but it is still a good deal for an agent with time on his or her hands.

Listing agents or specialists are a good hire, because it allows them to replace you in the field. I have an excellent listing presentation that sellers can relate to. They see the value of what I'm bringing to the table with my marketing plan. Once I train a good listing specialist on how to present that, they can take it and go out in the field. The listing agent orders the signs, hires the photographer to take the pictures, makes sure all the advertising is in place, and prepares all of the paperwork for the support staff in the office. After that, they follow up on showings, answer any questions the seller may have, set up the inspections, and schedule the closing. Sometimes they even go to the closing. The listing agent plays a key role because they build a relationship with the seller and the seller knows that they can reach out to that person to get all their questions answered. This helps me leverage my time and is a good way for the listing agent to make money at a flat 15 percent commission rate.

Today, I only use showing and listing agents for my own personal database and concentrate most of my time helping my agents and coaching members grow their real estate businesses and teams. Agents at Miranda Real Estate Group have very competitive compensation plans and have options on getting 100 percent of their commissions once they reach a certain amount of production. We still provide plenty of buyer and seller leads to our agents through various company lead-generation systems.

I have built my business on a team concept because I believe having the right team on board creates an excellent culture for my business. Craig Proctor taught me about the DISC personality test many years ago. It determines what type of personality your team members are and where they best fit in your organization. The four personalities identified are:

D - Dominant. *These folks are focused on getting results. They are direct and competitive.*

I - Influential. *These employees will have a lot of enthusiasm. They are friendly and optimistic.*

S - Steady. *These people are sincere, patient, and modest. They tend to be supportive by nature.*

C - Compliant. *These workers will be accurate and cautious. They are detailed with numbers and like things in a certain order.*

Dominant or Influential types make better salespeople. They are more competitive, more direct, and quicker to the punch. Steady and Compliant types may take a little bit more time and be more accurate. Anytime I am looking for someone to do more administrative roles, I am always looking for that S/C personality combination, because they make great support people. D and I people are better hires for the selling process. In the end, you want a combination of both. You don't want an unbalanced team.

A lot of times when you are hiring someone, you want to hire the opposite of yourself. So in my case, I'm a D/I personality type. I am pretty strong at sales—working with people and getting to the finish line to make the sale. I don't have the patience to waste an hour on paperwork or read a 60-page prospectus on how something works. That's just not me. I need to get results more quickly. So I hire the opposite of myself to compliment my business. In that way, I can be out there working with sellers and buyers and getting the marketing side done, and that is what I love to do. At the same time, I have someone in-house who is managing the contracts and doing all the detail work that I don't like to do. It is important to know yourself—and hire accordingly.

My goal is to have a company where I have an awesome culture, with good people working in it who are happy and enjoying what they are doing.

I find that my real estate agents love working for the Miranda Real Estate Group because they get the best of both worlds. They have the independence of building their own business within my business, and they also benefit from the assistance of my support staff to help them manage their listings as well as marketing themselves, so they don't have to pay for these services out of pocket. They also have the opportunity for me to coach and train them to help build their business. Most coaches and trainers haven't had the experience and success that I have had in the real estate business. This is a huge benefit for any agent looking to join our company or for the agents who already work with us.

Take, for example, my inside salesperson. Each member of my team has access to my inside salesperson, whose job is to follow up on leads 40 hours a week. One of my team agents was driving around a neighborhood and ran across a For Sale by Owner sign. That agent made a couple of attempts to reach the owner. Unsuccessful in doing so, the agent gave that information to our inside salesperson, who called the seller eight to ten times over the next two weeks until she finally reached him on a Sunday afternoon.

Ironically, it was just after the seller had held his third open house and he was frustrated that he didn't have any prospective buyers walking through the home. My inside salesperson was able to convince him that he should talk to my agent about some of the marketing ideas we have to get homes sold for top dollar. She booked that appointment for the next day; my sales agent was able to list the property and sold it within seven days, making a $7,000 commission—a commission he would never have received if it hadn't been for the inside salesperson being so tenacious in making her follow-up calls.

Once you start growing your team to the point where it becomes very profitable, it is important to keep a vision of what you want that team to look like. Don't just say you want a team and start hiring people. Sit down, take a few days, and write out exactly what you want your team to look like. Outline all the job descriptions of people you will eventually need on your team, and from there, spell out the vision for your team's growth. Then share that vision with the people currently on your team. Establish annual goals and break them down into quarterly, weekly, and daily objectives. Working in that structured manner has allowed our team to function together as a true team and share in the success of the company as we hit our goals.

I also hold daily huddles that meet for 15 minutes each day so that every team member knows exactly what is going on. It is especially critical for the support staff to know what files are coming in, what is closing for the day, and any challenges that must be addressed immediately. Then I hold a longer weekly meeting where we go into more detail on numbers and certain objectives that we are trying to accomplish. In this meeting, we look at our systems and processes to see what we can improve upon. I convene offsite quarterly meetings to talk about our annual objectives for the year. What is working, and more importantly, what is *not* working? What changes are needed going into the second quarter to get us back to where we need to be to guarantee we hit our annual goals. These quarterly meetings are essential because so many businesses set up annual goals in January, but by January 15, 90 percent of those goals, like New Year's resolutions, are forgotten and never looked at again.

I have met a lot of wonderful people in this business, many of them being real estate agents who have the potential to have very successful businesses, but they don't because they are afraid to give up control. If you are going to grow a successful business, then you cannot do it alone. You need to be able to hire the right people; you need to treat those people right, to train them appropriately, to build a terrific culture where your people feel good about the job that you are all doing together. If you can do that, you will have a very profitable and rewarding business.

CHAPTER 6

· ·

SELLING HOMES: THE STRATEGY OF SUCCESS

When I first started in real estate, I was told that open houses were a great way to meet new buyers. I remember doing open houses every weekend, sometimes two on Sundays. It was a lot of work preparing for them and it took Sundays away from my family, but it was definitely a good way for me to meet new clients. I had always viewed listings, especially in the beginning, as hard to obtain. A lot of agents mentioned how hard it was to get listings and that buyers represented more of the "now" business in real estate. If you were working with a motivated buyer, they were more likely to want to buy it *now* versus having to spend money investing in a listing that could take several months to sell.

Listings require an investment of your time, energy, and marketing dollars. You have to market those listings, and they could go six months or more and never sell. You need to have a certain expertise in order to take listings and know how best to price them right from the start. So for my first six months in the business, I tended to stay more with buyers.

Then one day it hit me that the agents who focused primarily on obtaining listings were better able to leverage their time. I noticed some of the more successful agents concentrated most of their time on listings and would have other people sell homes on their behalf.

I decided this was something I had to learn. There was some training available, and one of the big takeaways that I received from one of the old timers in the business was that you have to list to last. He actually told me one day, "You know, Willie, *you have to list to last in the real estate business.*" I never forgot that statement.

My first listing was from a friend of mine who was looking to relocate, and he needed to sell his house. I remember filling out the paperwork, going through his house and getting pictures, bringing them back to the office, and uploading them into the Multiple Listing Service. Three days later, I had the buyers of other agents calling me to show them the property, and they ended up bringing me an offer. Listings homes seemed much easier, and my focus now was to get more listings.

We were in a seller's market (see author's note at end of chapter) at the time, so all I really had to do was get homes on the market. Homes were selling within two or three weeks, as long as they were priced right. When I saw how easy it was, I decided to concentrate more on listings as I moved forward in my career.

I found I was able take on more clients by working with listings, and I was able to leverage my time better versus working with buyers out in the field. So I could easily carry 20–25 listings, where I couldn't easily grind out more than eight to ten buyers.

Listing Plan for
WMJ - Team Listing Plan

Activity	Description	Day	From	Reminder	Drop off	Assigned to
To-do	Add to CIREB (if applicable)	0	After listing date	0		Julie Riccio
To-do	Launch grad pricing (if applicable)	0	After listing date	0		Julie Riccio
To-do	Post to Craigslist	0	After listing date	0		Julie Riccio
To-do	Put in Homes.com	0	After listing date	0		Julie Riccio
To-do	Order Sign	0	After listing date	0		Julie Riccio
To-do	Add text rider to Excel sheet	0	After listing date	0		Julie Riccio
To-do	Check for Contact in Agent Office	0	After listing date	0		Julie Riccio
To-do	Update ShowingTime.com	0	After listing date	0		Julie Riccio
To-do	Check for Contact in Top Producer	0	After listing date	0		Julie Riccio
To-do	Ask Agent if having OH	0	After listing date	0		Julie Riccio
To-do	Add "Active Listing" to category	0	After listing date	0		Julie Riccio
To-do	Load listing to MLS	0	After listing date	0		Julie Riccio
To-do	Save listing pw to Active Listing folder	0	After listing date	0		Julie Riccio
To-do	Assign & log lockbox in Excel & TP	0	After listing date	0		Julie Riccio
To-do	Upload docs to MLS	0	After listing date	0		Julie Riccio
To-do	Review File	0	After listing date	0		Julie Riccio
To-do	Send Partially Loaded Listing To LA Fo...	0	After listing date	0		Julie Riccio
To-do	Add to Success website	0	After listing date	0		Julie Riccio
To-do	Add to Contest Tracking Sheet if Applic...	0	After listing date	0		Julie Riccio
To-do	Review MLS sheet	0	After listing date	0		Julie Riccio
To-do	Save photos to Active Photos folder	0	After listing date	0		Julie Riccio
To-do	Post to Postlets	0	After listing date	0		Julie Riccio
To-do	Assign SMS text rider	0	After listing date	0		Julie Riccio
To-do	Opt client out of Infusionsoft	0	After listing date	0		Tina Ryder
To-do	Email MLS sheet to team	0	After listing date	0		Julie Riccio
To-do	Verify USDA eligible	0	After listing date	0		Julie Riccio
To-do	Add AGL/CGL to user define field	0	After listing date	0		Julie Riccio
To-do	Add client contact info to TP	0	After listing date	0		Julie Riccio
To-do	Create www.RealEstateShows.com	0	After listing date	0		Julie Riccio
To-do	Enter text rider to user define	0	After listing date	0		Julie Riccio
To-do	Mail leave behind (if applicable)	1	After listing date	0		Julie Riccio
To-do	Print reports & contract for leave behind	1	After listing date	0		Julie Riccio
To-do	Verify Plan To-Do's Are Complete	3	After listing date	0		Tina Ryder
To-do	Verify property is on Zillow	3	After listing date	0		Julie Riccio
To-do	Notify Agent to call for reduction	30	After listing date	0		Julie Riccio
To-do	Repost to Postlets	58	After listing date	0		Julie Riccio
To-do	Notify Agent to call for reduction	60	After listing date	0		Julie Riccio
To-do	Notify Agent 90+ days on market	90	After listing date	0		Tina Ryder
To-do	Notify Agent to call for reduction	90	After listing date	0		Julie Riccio
To-do	Repost to Postlets	116	After listing date	0		Julie Riccio
To-do	Notify Agent to call for reduction	120	After listing date	0		Julie Riccio
To-do	Notify Agent to call for reduction	150	After listing date	0		Julie Riccio
To-do	Repost to Postlets	174	After listing date	0		Julie Riccio

What are some ways to obtain listings? There are several, and the best way, I feel, is with personal referrals. Real estate agents surveyed by the National Association of Realtors report that 67 percent of their listings came from referrals from past clients, friends, or family members. You can get personal referrals from your center of influence, by networking, or from your own personal database.

Another way to attract sellers is by having current listings. As soon as a "Sold" sign goes up on a house, that prompts other sellers in the neighborhood who were thinking about selling to say, "That guy Willie Miranda just had two listings in this neighborhood that sold fairly quickly. When it's time for us to sell our property, we're going to call Willie." Listings are important because seller listings create exposure, bringing in more buyer and seller leads to you. Every listing that's marketed correctly should generate one or more buyer sales from it. By having listings, you can definitely leverage yourself better because you are able to pick up buyers and sell the listing.

The key to success in working with listings is that you really need to show clients how you are different, how you are going to market their property, and how you are going to create more demand for their property by attracting more buyers to their home.

I developed a good, solid listing presentation. In that presentation, I tell my sellers that it comes down to three things that are going to sell their home fast and for top dollar: cleanliness, marketing, and price. If their home is in showroom condition, is taken care of, is clean, and doesn't have a lot of pet odors, that's going to be an ideal listing for me to be able to market and get sold.

The second key ingredient is marketing. Just sticking a sign on the lawn and posting the home on the Multiple Listing Service is not a good marketing plan for any seller. So I show them how I am able to generate more buyers through my print and online advertising plans and through my pool of ready-to-act buyers already in my "buyers in waiting" system.

We then discuss the importance of a strategic plan that includes pricing their home correctly right from the start. Ninety percent of any great marketing plan is having the right price. Many times when I was in a competitive situation with other agents and lost listings to them, it was because those agents overpriced the homes. It's what we call in our profession "buying the listing" by increasing the sales price. So if you have a client whose home was appraised at $300,000, another agent could come by and say that he or she could easily get $350,000 for that home. Clients would get that greedy look in their eye and say, "I'm going to go list with this other agent because he's going to get me $350,000, and Willie, you said we would only be able to sell it for $300,000."

I like to handle that objection up front and explain to the client what "buying a listing" means. I also review all the research, time, and energy that most people do up front today because they can find everything online. I tell them that I hope they are not going to pick their agent based on who gives them the best price but rather by who will market their home best to bring in more qualified buyers for their property.

As professionals, I feel it is our obligation to do the proper research and to explain to the seller what their home is worth based on the other comparable homes that have sold in the last six months to a year. So I have developed a 14-step process that has been very effective in winning the listings and selling homes for me.

Prior to a listing appointment, I'll send out a personal note with my professional brochure that tells them about my background. I also send them a prelisting packet that includes client testimonials and marketing materials that show them some of the ways that I promote my properties. I like to send that out first because it helps to set me apart from other agents when I go to that appointment.

THE 14-STEP LISTING PROCESS:

1. BE ON TIME.

It amazes me how many agents show up to listing appointments 15–20 minutes late. I have had sellers say to me, "We're not going to go with this other person because he or she was 20 minutes late and didn't even apologize when they finally did show up."

Sellers are turned off by tardiness and with good reason. Selling a home is probably the biggest financial transaction that sellers will go through. They are nervous, especially if they are relocating or if they have been in the same house for many years, and now they have to sell because they are downsizing or can't afford the home anymore. If they set up an appointment with you for 2 p.m. on a Sunday afternoon, you'd better be there before 2 p.m. that afternoon, because I guarantee you that by 1:30 p.m. the seller is pacing around the house and looking out the windows for you. They have spent a lot of time getting everything ready on their property, cleaning up the home, and landscaping, and by five minutes until 2 p.m., they are at the door watching for you and wondering where you are. At five after 2 p.m., they are stewing, their face is red, they are upset, and they are calling you to find out whether or not the appointment is still on. If you come strolling in at a quarter past 2 p.m., there is a good chance that you just lost a lot of credibility with that client. Try to get to the home five to ten minutes early if you can so that you are not rushed. This gives you time to look around the outside of the house or drive around the neighborhood to look at other houses, especially if you have other comparable homes that you need to see in the neighborhood. But at the very least, you definitely don't want to be late.

You also want to make sure that you are prepared. There is nothing worse than that seller looking out his or her window when you pull up. Having them see you run to the back of your trunk to grab a file, computer and then run back into the front seat to grab a pen, papers flying out of your hands. You want to make sure you are prepared prior to getting to the home, so you can look as professional as possible once you arrive and not a "hot mess."

2. KNOCK ON THAT DOOR, RING THAT DOORBELL.

And make sure that when you walk into the home you introduce yourself with a firm handshake, and look the seller in the eye. Let them know it is nice to meet them, and from there, ask to set up your laptop, iPad, or presentation binder. It is very important for you to take direction on, or select, the best location to present from. From my experience, the kitchen or dining room table works best. Try to avoid couches and areas without a table. Too often, I have had sellers say that an agent came in who couldn't look them in the eye or didn't shake their hand, or worse yet, gave them a wimpy handshake. You want to inspire confidence by giving them a firm handshake, making eye contact, having an inviting smile, and asking where you can go and set up.

3. MAKE SMALL TALK.

As you are setting up and getting your presentation up on the screen, make some small talk. You can chat about the neighborhood or the weather or whatever you want to talk about, but make a little bit of small talk. As nervous as you may be, depending on how long you have been in the business, that seller is even more nervous, and they want to break the ice with you as well.

4. ASK FOR A "QUICK" TOUR OF THE HOUSE.

You don't want an hour-long walk-through of their home; you want a quick tour. Ask them if it would be okay to take a look at their property with them. Be sure that when you take a quick tour around their house you have a notebook or pad of paper with you. Because when they are going through their house telling you all the wonderful things about it, you want to make notes to show that you are taking an interest in their property.

I remember going through a home early in my career, and when it came down to the listing, I asked the seller why she was giving me the listing versus the other agent she had interviewed. She answered, "You looked like you really cared about our property. You said you liked our house and that you knew it would sell, and you just took a lot more interest in it."

I asked if she could give me an example. She said, "You actually went through and wrote down the updates we told you we had done to the house. We spent over $100,000 updating this home over the last five years, and there were a lot of things we want a potential buyer to know, and you actually took notes on that." So having a pad of paper and taking copious notes of the home is a must-do on every listing appointment.

5. NEVER POINT OUT NEGATIVE SELLING DETAILS TO A SELLER.

It is just not a good way to build a relationship in the first few minutes of meeting with the seller. Some sellers can get very defensive. Once, I had a new agent shadow me on a listing appointment. We weren't in the house five minutes before the agent said, "What's that smell? Do you have a cat?" And the seller said, "Oh yes, we actually have two cats." And he said, "Oh. I can tell. I hate cats." That pretty much ended things right there. No matter what I said after that, the seller was extremely offended. She was a cat lover, and he came in there and said that the house smelled and that he hated cats. We had no shot at getting that listing.

So during the tour, say something positive, perhaps that the backyard is a good size or that they have decorated the home beautifully. Talk more on the positive side and only make mental notes of the negative selling points. Leave those negative selling points until the end of the presentation, when you give them tips on what they need to do to get their home ready for sale. Chances are they already know what needs to be done and will bring them up to you to get your opinion once they feel more comfortable with you.

6. COMPLIMENT THEM ON THE CONDITION OF THE HOME.

Let them know they have a great home and that they will have no problem selling it. Be sincere in what you are saying. Remember, the seller at this point is anxious, as most sellers don't think that their home will sell. They don't think what they have is of value, so who would come in and pay $200,000–$300,000 for their home? Their primary worry is that no one will like their home or want to buy it. By using that one statement, "You have a lovely home and you'll have no problem selling it," I have had many sellers thank me. They feel better because they know that we sell many homes in the area and that we are the real estate experts.

7. ASK WHAT THEIR MOVING PLANS ARE.

It is important to establish a time frame for their move. Find out what their goals are. Ask them key questions as to why they are moving, when they have to be there, and what they feel their home is worth. Also, find out how quickly they could move if their home sold in a week. Would they possibly need temporary housing, or would they have to wait five months down the road until little Johnny was out of school?

Discuss their financing to make sure they are not upside down on their home and are current with their mortgage payments. Once you have all that information, have established their motivation and timing for selling, and feel confident the sellers are ready to move forward and sell their home, then launch into your listing presentation.

Every once in a while, you will find out that the sellers are just not ready to get their home on the market. There are things they weren't aware of that still need to be done to get their home ready for sale. I will be the first one to say, "Based on the information you have shared, selling your home now may not be a good time. Why don't you take care of the items we discussed and then I'll come back at a later date." Sellers really appreciate that. They are grateful that you took the time to listen to what their needs were and acknowledged that the timing might not be right for them. I have seen agents take the listing knowing the seller was not ready to sell and unfortunately waste both time and money when the seller decides to withdraw their listing because they realize selling was not the best option for them at that time.

8. SEGUE INTO THE LISTING PRESENTATION.

Reiterate that there are three very important elements in selling a home: cleanliness, marketing, and price. Make sure they understand that their home must be clean, decluttered, and in pristine showing condition at all times. Perhaps the home is in perfect shape, but they just need to declutter a few things from the basement, clean out some closets, get the carpets cleaned, and do a little landscaping. Keep it to a couple of quick action items that you think will make a big difference in marketing their home. Most of the time, I find that sellers are already aware of these points and indicate them to me as we are going through the initial home tour. So I will just remind them about what they had said to me: "You mentioned the backyard needed to be cleaned up and that you wanted to paint that bedroom from bright red to a more neutral color. I definitely agree with you that those are things you'll definitely want to take care of prior to putting your home on the market."

From there, I'll say, "You also need extensive marketing to attract potential qualified buyers to your home. So I'm going to show you what we do at Miranda Real Estate Group to bring in qualified buyers to buy your home." I go through my listing presentation on my iPad, which includes background on my company and on my team approach. I have some client testimonials to show them, as well as a slide show that talks about the different community charity organizations I participate in. Then, I unveil how we market our properties. I show them our 17-step process, from placing the home in the Multiple Listing Service and other websites to all the different print advertising and media we do to market their home to sell fast and for top dollar.

When I reach the end of the presentation, I ask them if they have any questions about our marketing program. If they don't, I say, "Okay, let's move on to the pricing of your home, which is what we call a cost market analysis."

9. PULL OUT THE COST MARKET ANALYSIS.

Show them a range of homes you have selected based on active, pending, and sold listings. Give them a snapshot of what is happening in their market area and explain to them the criteria you used to come up with the estimate. I like to show the inside photos of these comparable homes so the seller gets a good idea of what the other homes had to offer. This is a very important step, as sellers will start realizing what their home is really worth and what buyers are willing to pay for homes in the current market.

10. EXPLAIN WHAT THE COST MARKET ANALYSIS IS.

Start with the active listings. These are homes they will be in competition with. Explain that these prices are sometimes overpriced (I often refer them as Fantasy Land), because anyone can put up whatever they want as a price when they list their home. You just want them to know the homes that are out there, so that when someone is looking for a four bedroom, two-and-a-half bath, two-car garage Colonial in a certain price range, they are aware of the homes that they are competing with. If homes are priced and marketed correctly, they should be getting good activity and an offer within the first 30 days.

The second category you want to circle and point out are the listings that are currently pending. These are homes that have recently sold, and are still under contract. You don't know what the actual sold price is yet, but the key indicator here is that you do know what the listing price was at the time an offer came through.

The third column you want to show them is the closed sales. This is "reality." This is the column that you want them to pay close attention to because these are the homes that have officially closed, and this is the best way to determine the market value of their property. It doesn't matter what their friend sold her house for three years ago in the neighborhood. It doesn't matter what the person next door has listed his home for. None of that matters. The only thing that matters are closed sales, because it is the only thing that matters to the bank. Most banks will only go back three to six months of closed-sale activity. So it is important to focus your efforts on closed sales in your listing presentation. At the end of the day, your home is only worth what a buyer is willing to pay for it.

11. MATCH CLOSED SALES TO THE SELLER'S HOME.

Review features, square footage, and other amenities that are in the home. Look at the sales prices and days on the market. Consider the number of bedrooms and baths. Look at their property, and then look at the next four to five homes that best match theirs within a radius of where their home sits. Go on the Internet and show them inside photos of those properties. Show them what the houses originally listed at, what they were reduced to, and what they eventually sold for.

This really opens the eyes of a lot of sellers who thought their home was worth a certain amount. Looking at all the prices for which these homes have sold for, some possibly for much lower than what they thought their home was worth, puts sellers more in touch with reality as to what their home's true value is in today's market.

12. ASK THEM WHAT THEY THINK THEIR HOUSE IS WORTH.

Be direct. After looking over these recent home sales, ask where they feel their home should be priced. Then keep your mouth shut. You never want to give the seller the exact price because it doesn't matter what price you feel or an appraiser says the home is worth; it is only worth what a buyer is willing to pay. The best you can do is to give them a range and then wait to hear what they say. Sometimes at that point they'll say, "You know what? I was thinking $325,000 to start, but now that you showed me all these different properties and that the market is a little bit lower than I thought. Maybe pricing under $300,000 would be best." Or people say, "Gee, I didn't think it was worth that much. I'm pretty happy, because it's worth more money than I believed."

But you never want to give the price of the home to the seller first, because if they hear a price that they don't like, they are not going to hear anything else you say moving forward. Now they can't wait for you to get out of their house, because in their mind, you are not going to be able to help them get the price that they really want.

13. AGREE ON A PRICE.

Based on how the conversation goes with the seller, determine what they feel they should receive for their home and what they would like to list it for. Point out to the sellers that buyers usually look at homes in $25,000 increments. So if you have a home that you really feel strongly is worth under $300,000, I'll push for that seller to price it at $299,900, because if they list it above $300,000, let's say at $309,900 to start, they're going to be missing out on a lot potential buyers who might be only looking up to the $275,000–$300,000 range, which is really the right buyer for their home.

14. CLOSE FOR THE LISTING.

After agreeing on the price of the home, you need to close for the listing. Sit down with the seller and say, "I went over our aggressive marketing program with you, and I am confident we can get your home sold for top dollar and with the least amount of hassle. Are you ready to list your home with me today?" Again, keep your mouth shut, as the first person that talks usually loses. If they are a ready, motivated seller, your only reason for going on that appointment is to walk out of there with the listing paperwork. You don't want to go to sellers' homes and do all the work for them so they can go and list with another agent. You are going there because you want to get that listing paperwork completed and get their home on the market.

In some cases, people are not ready to list, and that's okay. We know they are going to be listing down the road, maybe in three to six months, and that's okay too. But if someone is looking to get their home sold and they are ready to get it on the market right then or within the next week or two, then you want to make sure that you ask for the business.

I have had sellers who say, "I really want to paint the room first, and get the carpets cleaned."

I say, "That's no problem. How long do you think it will take for you to do that?" They'll tell me a week or two weeks.

Then I say, "Well, today is the first of the month. Will you be ready by the 15th of the month?"

And if they say, "Oh yes, definitely by that time, the 15th of the month should be no problem," then I suggest getting the paperwork out of the way now and just dating it for the 15th. Remind them that as it gets closer to that date, they can always change it if they have to. But at least you can start doing the pre-listing prep work now and put the marketing in place for them, so that come the 15th, you can come out of the gate strong and get their home listed right away. Eighty percent of the time, sellers will agree to that. The point is that you have to *ask for the listing.*

Regarding commissions, I recall a mentor that I had a lot of respect for who always obtained high commissions. Where other agents would negotiate and lower their commissions just to get the listing, this man told me he never negotiated his commissions. "That's one of the things I don't do," he said. I asked how he could do that when he was in competition, and he answered, "Willie, remember this, cost is only an issue in the absence of value." He had a process where he never talked commission with a client until he went through everything he does for them as far as marketing and all of the added value he was able to provide them. He showed his clients the value of what he brought to the table and why a seller should choose him versus any other agent. Because he was able to do this so effectively, he always received top dollar. I never forgot that: *Cost is only an issue in the absence of value.*

Practice really does make perfect. You get one shot to make a good impression. You can stand out from the competition with a good listing presentation. You really need to show the sellers your entire marketing program and how you are going to get their home sold by creating the most demand for their home. In the end, the seller will always go with who they know, like, and trust the most, but also with who is educating them through the process. Your commission rate will not be a factor because if you show them that you are adding a lot more value than the average agent, clients will always select you and never beat you up on your commission. Well, let's just say most of the time!

AUTHOR'S NOTE:

- A "seller's market" is when the demand is larger than the supply. People have more money to spend on real estate, so sellers will often see several buyers competing to buy their property, which drives up the price. This means that buyers will have to spend more to get what they want. This is the ideal situation for sellers, because they get a great price on their homes.

- A "buyer's market" is what you get when there is more supply than demand. There are more people looking to sell homes than there are people looking to buy homes. In a buyer's market, sellers may have to accept a lower price than they want to sell their home and may have to resort to staging and incentives. This is the ideal situation for buyers, because they can usually get a great deal on a home.

CHAPTER 7

. . . .

WORKING WITH BUYERS: THE SELLING OF SUCCESS

There are really two distinct sides of any real estate transaction: the buying side or the listing side.

In 1998, when I first earned my real estate license, I was told that I had to knock on doors, make cold calls, and do open houses to get business. So I volunteered on my first week in the business to do an open house and I met a nice young couple. They had a one-year-old and another baby on the way. The husband had a job, and the wife was laid off at the time, but they definitely seemed very motivated to purchase a home. So I was excited to have a client that wanted to work with me to buy a home.

They weren't interested in the home they looked at for the open house. It was over their budget and too big for them. So I researched a good 15 to 20 homes for them, and we set up appointments over the next three weeks to view every one of them. We finally ran across a property that they were really interested in. It was time to write my first offer.

I met with my manager and told her the situation. She gave me the forms to fill out for the contract, and I filled in all of the blanks. When it was done, my manager looked at it and said, "Where's the pre-qualification letter from the lender?" And I said, "I didn't know we needed that." She replied, "It's one of the first steps you need to take before you work with a buyer. You should have had the pre-qualification letter done beforehand." We had to delay the actual presentation of the contract because we needed to call the lender the next morning.

We called the lender the next day, and my client gave them all the financial information the lender needed over the phone. The lender called us back a couple of hours later and said, "Sorry, but your buyer is not qualified to buy a home at this time. They had a bankruptcy and a car repossession within the last 12 months, and that disqualified them."

So I wasted countless hours showing homes to these potential buyers—time away from my family—*assuming* that this family could buy a home, only to find out that they weren't qualified. I promised myself that I would never do that again. That was a big life lesson I learned, and I now know that I need to put together a good process when working with buyers.

Today, my first objective in working with buyers is to meet with them for a one-on-one fact-finding appointment. The goal of the fact-finding appointment is to determine whether or not this is, first and foremost, a qualified buyer, to get a good idea of what they are looking for, and to establish their timing and motivation for buying.

Many buyers out there want to buy a home, but life gets in the way and they may be ahead of themselves. Or some people should have bought a home five or ten years ago and were never shown just how to do it.

I tell my buyers that purchasing a house is not an event that you just show up to; it is an actual process. And the first step of that process is to come into my office, and meet with me. I am not resistant to meeting clients at their homes if that is more convenient, but by having them come to my office I find that I am better able to control the environment, and there are fewer distractions.

When I sit down with them for the one-on-one appointment, I follow a two-page sheet that collects some basic information: their name, email address, cell phone, and contact information, and then I have a list of 15 questions. Some of those questions include: Why do they want to buy a home? What areas do they want to live in? Is the school district something that is important to them? How many bedrooms do they need? What are their future family plans? How long do they anticipate staying in that property?

These are just some of the questions that I ask, which are important. I have had buyers come into my office who quickly become non-buyers when they grasp that they are not ready to buy a home or realize that they don't really know what they want in a home.

The objective is to get a good feel for what they are looking for and to make sure that I am not wasting my time working with a non-motivated buyer. If they aren't prequalified, I go through the prequalifying process with them. Many times, buyers will go out and find a house first, then try to get pre-qualified. As I mentioned earlier, that is really the wrong way of doing it. You want to make sure that a buyer is prequalified and that they are living within their means. Many buyers are able to qualify for a much higher loan that would strap them financially on their month-to-month cash flow.

Once I get a good feel for that and we have the prequalification done, then I will move forward with an extensive home search that meets their criteria. I want to give my buyers total control of the home-buying process by giving them all the homes that are currently for sale and that meet their home-buying criteria. In the past, if there were 30 or 40 homes that were available, we were trained to only show them eight or ten of those homes, under the belief that if you show too many homes to a buyer, they become confused, and a confused mind takes no action. I think that is the wrong approach. I give my clients information on all the available properties out there that meet their criteria, and let them go ahead and do the drive-bys first. Pictures that are posted online sometimes doesn't show the commercial exposure or the rundown, boarded-up house that is across the street. I tell them that when they drive by, they should look at the house and ask themselves, *Is this somewhere I could call home? Is it a neighborhood that I feel comfortable living in?* If it passes that test and it is something they want to get in to see, then I go ahead and set up an appointment.

Before I show them a property, I tell them, "We'll walk through every property that you want to see. When we go through these properties and you feel at any point that the house is not going to work for you or you just don't 'feel the love' for the home, you're not hurting my feelings by saying 'Willie, stop, this is not the house for me.'" I make it very clear that at any point in time if they feel the house is not for them, then we need to move on to the next property. That is the process I use when working with buyers.

To review: at that first buyer appointment, walk them through all the steps of the buying process (refer to www.freewilliestuff.com

for the buyer process flow sheet I use). Complete the buyer profile to determine if it is a go. If it is, sit with them and go through your buyer's presentation and show them the entire process of buying a home—from initially meeting with you, to viewing properties, to signing the contract, to getting their attorney, their inspector, and lender, right down to the closing table. Do a thorough job on all the significant things you want to focus on and getting them prequalified, making sure you search multiple listings and for sale by owners to show the right properties to them, and then negotiating the best price on their behalf.

After the presentation is done, have them sign a buyer agreement. The buyer agreement is something I find a lot of real estate agents don't do. Seventy-five percent of buyer agents don't have their clients sign a buyer agreement because they are afraid of rejection or afraid that the buyer won't sign, so they go ahead and show them properties without it.

That is a big mistake, because when I work with a buyer, I want to make sure that buyer is committed to me. If I am going to invest a lot of time and energy finding them the best home at the best price, then I want to make sure they are totally on board with me. That buyer agreement is an agreement between that buyer and myself that states we are going to be working together over the next six to twelve months. Whether the property is listed with the multiple listing agent or if it is a for sale by owner, that buyer has agreed to pay me a commission. Most real estate agents would never list a property without a listing agreement. So I don't understand why agents wouldn't sign a buyer client to a buyer agreement.

Once they find a home, the rest of the process goes pretty smoothly. We write up the contract and have an attorney review it to make sure it is in the buyer's best interest. Then we go ahead and get the inspections done. A home inspection is something that I always go to with my buyers, and if I can't be available, then I will have my licensed assistant go to the inspection on my behalf. Even if the buyer feels that there is nothing wrong with the home or it is a newer home, I encourage them to get an inspection done, because you never know what will come up once they own that home. I don't want them coming back to me upset because they bought a home that has black mold in the attic or has a furnace that doesn't work properly or worse yet, a home that has pests, such as termites or carpenter ants.

Often, people don't want to do septic inspections because they feel if the owners have had the septic tank for a long time, then it is running fine. And it does cost $300 or more to get a septic inspection done. But I have had buyers thank me afterward because the septic system did have something wrong with it, and they were able to get the seller to give them a credit at closing in order to fix it after the closing.

When the inspections are completed, I make sure there is nothing else that must be negotiated. Every once in a while, there might be a bad roof or a furnace that is not working correctly. If that is the case, I will have a professional come in and give the buyer an estimate, and we will try to negotiate by having the seller repair it or by giving us a credit, at least providing a partial payment for what it would cost to replace it.

When a buyer asks me, "What do you think we should offer for this house?" I will answer, "We should offer them a fair price, and the fair price is going to be determined by me doing a cost market analysis on that property." If it is a three-bedroom ranch, then I am going to look at all other three-bedroom ranches in the area to determine what those homes sold for. That will give us a good idea of what the current market value is on that home. I always have them offer on the lower end of the range, and then go from there.

One of the strategies that I like the best in negotiating a price is having the buyer write a letter or tape a video email to the seller, letting them know why they selected their home, how they felt the minute they walked into it, and how excited they are about purchasing their home. I have had them submit pictures of their family with the offer, to show them their sincere interest, including a note that says something like, "We have been looking for a safe neighborhood like this. Your home has a pool, it has everything that we wanted in a home, and as soon as we walked through your house, we felt this was the perfect home for us. This is why we hope that you will accept our offer." I call it the "buyer love letter" and it works pretty well, especially in multiple offer situations.

One time, I took a buyer I was representing to go see a farmhouse. It was a nice home. The people that lived there had lived there for 40 years, raised their family there, and were well known in the neighborhood. They were downsizing and moving to Florida. My buyer loved the house and wanted to purchase the home. But another buyer from New York City was coming up and offering $10,000 above their offer.

Since I was able to actually present my buyer's offer in person, I also brought a letter from my buyer. "They really loved your home." I said. They're a nice young family just starting out and I know you have a higher offer, but if you would really consider their offer I think you'll be selling it to a great family." The seller took our offer, $10,000 less, because they wanted a nice family to take over their home.

Over the years of negotiating home sales, I have come to realize that not all real estate transactions are business transactions. There is definitely an emotional transaction taking place as well for sellers, especially those who have lived in their homes for 20-plus years, raised their families there, and hold many memories in that home. Selling their home is a big step in life. It is an emotional transaction for them. It isn't just about the money. But on my end it is *more of* a business transaction. My job is to get the buyer the best price that I can for the best home that meets their needs without getting my emotions in the way. That is why they hired me.

If you are a new agent, working with buyers is a solid sales pillar of any real estate business. Like I said, buyers represent "now" business and in many ways are more profitable than listing homes. The reason is that when you list homes, you must spend a lot of upfront money in marketing, time, advertising, and expenses, and six months down the road that property may still never sell. When you are working with a buyer, basically you are investing your time. And you can get paid a lot sooner if you find a motivated buyer who is already prequalified. If you find the right properties for them, you could be under contract within a week and, hopefully, have a commission check in your pocket four to six weeks down the road. However, when you list a property, it can take double or triple that time to get paid if and only if that property sells. So that is the benefit of working with buyers.

A great advantage to working with buyers is they tend to know others and have friends who are also in the market to buy homes. This is an excellent way to obtain new referrals. Their reticular activators are at a peak state, creating an opportunity to obtain referrals. From my experience, the goal is to receive two referrals from each buyer while you are servicing that buyer. In addition, staying in touch with these buyers will pay off because eventually these buyers will outgrow their homes or look to relocate down the road. That is why it is essential to communicate with the buyer not only during the sales process but also after the sale of the home or the purchase of the home in order to get their repeat/referral business in the future.

There is a saying real estate agents have: "buyers are liars." It stems from the feeling that buyers will work with a real estate agent only until they get frustrated with the process, because if there is no commitment to them and no agreement in place, the buyer is free to use any real estate agent. Or if they are online looking at a property, they may go ahead and buy a house on their own or with another agent.

If you use the process that I outlined in this chapter, following it step by step, buyers are in fact, *not* liars. Buyers can be good and profitable clients. If used correctly, buyer clients will be very lucrative for your business and will give you repeat and referral business for years to come.

CHAPTER 8

· ·

TESTIMONIALS: THE
WORDS OF SUCCESS

Testimonials are an extremely important part of the success of your business and your relationship-building journey in real estate. They will elevate your reputation, your visibility, your credibility, and your trustworthiness. Not using testimonials in their marketing is a big mistake most real estate agents make, even though they are not that hard to obtain.

WHAT EXACTLY IS A TESTIMONIAL?
· ·

Testimonials are written or recorded statements that support your credibility and level of expertise. They also strengthen your reputation by expressing the trust that other people have in you and your business. They can help you attract deeper interest from prospective clients and existing clients that will make your business increasingly more successful.

WHY ARE TESTIMONIALS SO IMPORTANT?

When it comes to all businesses, large or small, the success of the business depends heavily on word of mouth. Testimonials are a formal form of expression that supports that concept. They are a powerful tool in strengthening your brand and the credibility of you and your business. As I have stated repeatedly, people do business with who they know, like, and trust ... and find to be credible. You will be surprised at how many valuable testimonials you will be able to collect just by asking your clients directly for them.

WHAT IS THE MOST EFFECTIVE WAY
TO OBTAIN TESTIMONIALS?

Anytime you have a positive interaction with a buyer or a seller in a real estate transaction, that is a perfect opportunity to ask for a testimonial. You can ask for these testimonials right at your initial client meeting or anytime during your interactions with them. At the listing presentation, ask for a testimonial by saying, "If and when I do a good job for you, I hope that you will tell your friends and family members the same, so I am going to make sure that I do a good job for you."

As we are going through the process of the transaction, I'll talk about obtaining a testimonial from them. "I really want to continue doing a good job for you. Selling you a home is the highest priority for me so that you will recommend me to your friends and family."

Approximately 90 percent of the testimonials that I receive are either done at the closing or just after the closing has occurred. I bring a camera with me to get a picture of that client out in front of their home with a sold sign. Sometimes, I take a picture at the closing table that includes their family as well. If I am able to do so, I will also get in the picture, so people can connect me to that success story.

At the end of one client's closing when everything was done and everyone was shaking hands, and the check was exchanged, we went outside the conference room and found a nice background. My client, his wife, and their three-month-old baby held a "Sold" sign up, and we took a picture. It was a very happy time for them with a newborn baby and their first home, and that joy showed in the photo.

I let them know that I wanted to use their photo in my marketing and promotions for my company, if that was acceptable to them. They agreed, and I told them I would send them a copy of the photo as well. I then asked if they could give me a couple of kind words to use in a testimonial and provided them with some bullet points that reminded them of our transaction together. With that information, they typed out a nice testimonial for me and gave me their permission to use it in future marketing promotions.

Once I received that testimonial, I used social media to share it. Twenty years ago when the Internet wasn't available, testimonials were all word of mouth. Now, whether it is buying a pair of shoes, buying a new car, or going to a restaurant, everyone is online searching for endorsements. They want to see the reviews that are posted there. It is just as imperative to have positive reviews in the real estate business. In this situation, I posted their photo on Facebook and asked them if it would be okay if I tagged them, so the photo could go out to all of their friends. It also goes out to my network, so all of their friends and my friends would see it and know they had bought a home and had a positive experience *with* me. When I uploaded the photo, I added a post saying, "Congratulations to Mark and Mary Jones for purchasing this home at 123 Main Street. It's their first home, and I know Mary will love cooking for Mark in their new custom gourmet kitchen." Once I posted that, I asked Mark and Mary to comment on it. By doing so, it started the conversation with their friends and family members online.

The best part is that I was attached to that conversation, so I was able to view all of those comments. People posted, "You're so lucky, we can't sell our home, we've been on the market six months," or "We're next, and we want to find a nice home as well." I could then pick up on those comments and find leads in them. The idea is that it allowed me to penetrate their personal relationships just by putting a testimonial out there. The volume of testimonials that I am able to post on social media indicates the frequency with which I sell homes.

In 2003, I did a lot of television marketing of my listings. I would buy ten to fifteen minutes of air time on a local cable station and post all of my homes on there. I would show a picture of one house and the price and then go to the next house and the next one. My phone number would be shown for the entire time, and I would get calls from perspective buyers looking to see those properties.

Three years later, the cable station that I used no longer provided that service, so I decided to buy a 30-minute infomercial. In the infomercial, I talked about how I did business with our clients. I went over my listing presentation and talked about my marketing strategies and services. But I also wanted to utilize video testimonials. I wanted the audience to relate to my clients who were giving me the testimonials. If I were pursuing the senior market, I would have one of my older clients give a great testimonial about how I was able to help them downsize their home. If it were a family that owned a home they were outgrowing and wanted to move up to a larger home, then I would have a client I had helped with a trade-up situation tell their personal experience.

I wanted to get about 15 or 20 testimonials like this for my info-mercial. So I decided to have a client party in a very upscale restaurant. I called up my clients and invited them, saying, "I'm having a client appreciation event from 5 to 7 p.m. on Thursday night. I'd love for you to come down, have a glass of wine, and eat some good food. I'd also like you to help me in updating my marketing efforts." I then explained that I would have a videographer there to tape the event and that he would be available to take them off to the side and get a personal video testimonial from them. All I asked is that they shared some of their best experiences working with me and my team.

I was surprised that all 20 of the people I invited to the event that night agreed to do the video testimonial. I know some people are shy and not all that comfortable on camera, especially if it was going to air on television. They each gave great testimonials that I was able to use in various different media outlets, and I also created a 30-minute video for my website.

That 30-minute video says a lot about my marketing and what I do to get homes sold fast at top dollar with the least amount of stress. But let's face it; if I were just saying that, there would be a fair amount of skepticism out there. It would have a very "salesy" feel if I just talked about how great I was and what my company can do for our clients. But with video testimonials from real clients, it gives my message credibility. It says, "This is the real deal, because these are real life people." I feel real estate agents make a big mistake if they don't use testimonials in their business.

You can also use those video testimonials on your website, on your Facebook page, and other social media platforms. You can use them in what we call a series of email drip campaigns. For instance, I had recorded ten seller video testimonials and ten buyer video testimonials. I put them in a sequence in a drip campaign for any buyer prospect that came to my website. I would send them emails over a ten-week period. Each week, for ten weeks, they would get a different testimonial. I would give them some information and then say, "Hey! Take a look at what the Bahndaris had to say about our marketing, or take a look at what the Delgados had to say about our services." When they would click on that link, the video testimonial would pop up and play right over their computer or smartphone.

Postcards are probably one of the best print media formats that you can use to drum up real estate business, especially new listings. Instead of sending out a regular "Just Listed" or "Just Sold" postcard, I also incorporate a testimonial. I want it to be as specific as possible. For instance, there is a case study that I did where I was sending out a lot of information to a certain neighborhood and only getting one or two listings from that neighborhood per year. When I switched my marketing efforts and added testimonials to the marketing that I sent out, I saw my business more than quadruple in the number of sales within one year. The testimonials were from people whom I had done business with in that specific neighborhood.

The reason the marketing became more credible when I added a testimonial done by one of their neighbors was that it tied me to that community. People thought, "If Willie sold that house for the Smiths in only 17 days, Willie could probably sell ours as well." I have done a lot more sales in that neighborhood by using testimonials.

"Willie Came Through For Us...
When We Had Lost Hope."

"You will receive my upfront guarantee in writing that your home will sell fast at a price acceptable to you."

-Willie Miranda

We were relocating to another State for work and tried to sell our home For Sale By Owner for over 6 months with no results. We had heard good things about Willie's team and their Marketing, so we thought we would give them a call. We are so glad that we did. They were able to help us sell our home quickly and for the price we needed to complete our move. We wish we had called Willie sooner, but we are glad we finally did.

-The Munyans

To order a FREE SPECIAL REPORT
That explains how my unique and proven program will benefit you.
Call 518-348-2060 or visit www.12065HomeValue.com

MIRANDA
Real Estate Group, Inc.

If you do a good job for your clients and are sincere about what you do, your clients can become your biggest raving fans. As a result, they can return thousands and hundreds of thousands of dollars of increased revenue to your business.

Testimonials can make or break your business. The modern-day consumer goes online to look for information about you and your company. Therefore, it is vital to make sure you are giving exceptional service to people, because you cannot delete a lot of the written reviews that are done online. You have no control of them.

Yelp, Zillow, and Trulia are just a few websites where once the consumer posts something on their site about your company, you have no ability to remove that post. I had a situation a few years back where a seller was unhappy because one of my agents included their washer and dryer in the sale of their home. I was unaware of it, but my agent did know and never did anything about it.

This client was irate but instead of calling me, he tried to reach out to that agent numerous times and the agent said, "I'm sorry, the washer and dryer were included in the contract, and there's nothing I can do about it. Call your attorney."

Unfortunately, this upset individual went online and posted on 20 different consumer real estate websites on how awful his experience was with our company and how the company misrepresented the seller by including in the sales transaction personal items that belonged to him.

Given this information, I reached out to him to ask him as to why he was posting these negative comments and added that the agent was no longer at my company. He explained what had happened, and when I investigated the file, he was correct that the washer and dryer had been erroneously included in the sale of the home. I felt we owed that client a credit or reimbursement of that washer and dryer, and I took care of that for him.

The client appreciated the fact that I had gone above and beyond to take care of this issue for him. In return, he went back to all the different websites where he had posted negative reviews, took the reviews off, and replaced them with positive comments.

In every closing and every interaction that you have with a client, you should obtain a testimonial from that client. All you have to do is ask, and most clients will be more than happy to give you good testimonials as long as you did a good job for them and they felt they received excellent service. Getting testimonials is the most inexpensive marketing technique that you can use to enhance and grow your business multiple times over. Because once again, people want to do business with who they know, like, and trust, and testimonials are by far one of the best ways for them to articulate that to the average consumer who does not know you.

CHAPTER 9

. . . .

OPERATIONS: THE
SYSTEMS OF SUCCESS

I was 15 years old when I had my first experience with a true business operation. I got a job at the most famous franchise in the world today, McDonald's. I remember my first week on the job like it was yesterday. Downstairs in the basement of the restaurant, there were rows and rows of videotapes and three-ring binders, all labeled and all in order. I sat with two other employees and a shift manager at this little picnic table that had a VCR setup and a TV. The first day on the job we learned about the philosophy of the company, the company's vision and its mission statement, what McDonald's stood for, and how it was created. We spent an entire week downstairs in that basement studying all the different products that McDonald's had to offer.

Once we completed that portion of our training, they moved us upstairs to the main floor where my job was to make french fries. I spent a whole day with the shift supervisor at the french fry station. McDonald's had a certain procedure for putting the french fries in, pulling them out when the timer rang, shaking them, and salting them, and it was all done to the letter. Next, they promoted me to making hamburgers, and I figured that would be easy. After all, I had made hamburgers on the grill at my house—what was the big deal?

Well, that assumption went out the window as soon as the shift supervisor showed me how they made hamburgers at McDonald's. You had to put a certain number of hamburgers on the big grill in just the right order. The exact size hamburger had to be cooked at the exact temperature for an exact amount of time. A buzzer told you when to flip the hamburgers, when to put salt on them, when to add onions and cheese, and when to throw the buns into the oven in order to get them toasted just right. And that had a timer too!

Everything came out on time, and we were able to wrap that hamburger up and get it out to the customer, and then there was another system in place for how long that hamburger stayed out on the shelf. The point was they wanted to make sure that a hamburger made in Schenectady, New York, would taste exactly the same as a hamburger made in Los Angeles, California. No matter which McDonald's you went to, anywhere across the country, all the hamburgers tasted the same because of the systems and operations McDonald's put in place to create consistency and maintain quality among their franchises. McDonald's is one of the most successful franchises in the world and is basically run by teenagers who can't even make their beds in the morning. The reason for that is the systems and operations they have put in place.

In my first sales job after college with Prudential Financial Services, I noticed that there were also systems in the insurance business—systems for writing homeowners' policies and systems for underwriting life insurance policies. There were checklists and operation manuals galore at Prudential. But when I moved over to Allstate Insurance, while they had different manuals and procedures, they didn't have any checklists in place to process my new business files. So I began to develop what I called a "new business checklist." On that new business checklist, I itemized tasks I would need to complete whenever a prospect came in for an auto or homeowners' policy. I made sure I had all of their client information: their email addresses and supporting documents for compliance, such as a copy of their driver's license or a copy of their defensive driving certificates. This checklist made my life a lot easier. It let me deliver better customer service to my clients, and it allowed me to do more business because I was able to focus more of my valuable time on sales and not on chasing paperwork.

In my first year with Allstate, I became the number-one auto insurance writer in the upstate New York region, and I was asked to speak to a group of top Allstate agents across the state. When they wanted to know what my "secret sauce" was, I just held out my new business checklist and shared it with everyone. It became the highlight of that meeting, and since then I have talked to agents who still use that same checklist today, 20 years later. It made them more efficient and more accountable, and their production went up as well.

As a new real estate agent in 1998, I once again found myself in the position of needing to develop my own systems and checklists to make sure I was doing everything that I needed to be doing in working with buyers and sellers. As my business had begun to increase, I had become overwhelmed, misplacing documents and not delivering consistent service to my clients. I found myself working harder and harder to do the same things over and over again.

I decided to use what I had learned in the insurance business, so I put checklists in place for my real estate business. I started with the buyer side. Eighty percent of my business was working with buyers, so I put a buyer's checklist together. In that buyer's checklist, I would have information about the client: their full name, address, and phone numbers. It also identified the lead source and how I obtained that client.

This became the buyer profile. I would ask them key questions, such as what areas they wanted to live in, what school districts that they wanted to be in, and if they had a magic wand that could find their perfect house, what that house would look like.

Then I moved on to create a seller's checklist. I went through the seller's checklist in pretty much the same format as I did with the buyer's checklist, but the seller's checklist contained more detail, as more things needed to be done on the seller's side. I wanted to make sure that I not only collected all the proper paperwork but that I also obtained a copy of their tax bills, their deed, and their survey. The checklist went over specific information on the different amenities that they had in their home and highlighted what they loved most about it. By crafting these buyer and seller checklists, I was able to deliver high-quality service to my clients each and every time, and as a result, I picked up more and more referral business.

Checklist to Submit a listing

Property Address:_____

Client's Full Name:_____

Client's Email Address:_____

Client's Contact Phone #s:_____

Lead Source: _____ **Inside Sales: Yes or No   AGL or CGL:** _____

Marketing Materials: Yes or No - Mailed or Delivered: _____

Graduated Pricing: Yes or No

MANDATORY (Please note incomplete listing will not be processed)

1. _____ Key information   **Lockbox #**_____
2. _____ Exclusive Right to Sell Listing Agreement
3. _____ Sign Order Form
4. _____ ShowingTime Form
5. _____ ReInsight Tax Print Out
6. _____ Disclosure of Agency Relationships (Initialed on front & signed on back)
7. _____ Property Disclosure (If residential up to 3 family dwelling & seller agrees to complete)
8. _____ Disclosure to Seller Regarding Property Condition Disclosure
9. _____ Lead Base Paint Disclosure
10._____ Carbon Monoxide/Smoke Detector Disclosure
11._____ Affiliate Company Disclosure/**Exclusion from 90 Day Guaranteed Sales Program**

Preferred Documents To Be Submitted With Listing

12._____ Recent Paid Tax Bill (County & School, Village if applicable)
13._____ Copy of Executed Deed
14._____ Plot Plan or Survey
15._____ Miranda Graduated Pricing Addendum (If Applicable)
16._____ Miranda Cancellation Guarantee (If Applicable)
17._____ Bank Information If Short Sale Applies
18._____ Signed Bank Authorization If Short Sale Applies

Special Instructions or other needed info:

_____

_____

I remember at one point when I didn't have the checklist for the seller's side, a seller called me to ask why the "For Sale" sign wasn't up on his lawn. It was because I had totally forgotten to put it up. I had been really busy that week, with five or six listings that I had to input, and I never got out there to put a sign out on his lawn. I have had situations when we sold a home, and the new buyers would call and say, "Your sign is still up on my property. Come and get it," because I had forgotten to go and pick it up. Those things can be very embarrassing. It shows incompetence on the agent's part, and that results in not getting future business from that client.

In *The E-Myth Revisited*, Michael Gerber writes that there are many job roles we each play every day. In my case, the organizational chart began with me as CEO, but as I went through all the different things that I did, from administrative tasks to sales tasks to being a courier to going to closings, I realized that in order for me to grow, I would eventually need to leverage myself and fill that chart in with other people's names. Gerber emphasizes that there are three things that you need in order to be successful in your business: people, technology, and systems.

Working all on my own, I was the only "people" in that equation. I knew I would need to have other people take over some of those jobs. The technology was there. The Internet was alive, and there were many different online software programs available to make my business run more efficiently. I was eventually able to enter my checklists into software programs so that they became synchronized. Being able to put my own systems inside that technology allowed me to deliver consistent results that made a huge difference for my business. Michael Gerber underscores that "Once you have systems set up properly, you no longer need to manage people, you just need to have people to manage the systems. As long as the people follow the systems, you'll have a successful business." I was finding this to be true.

That is why McDonald's was so successful. As long as employees followed their systems to the letter, McDonald's all over the world would deliver consistent results. In the real estate business, there weren't many systems to follow, so I had to create my own. Over the years, I find myself continually tweaking and changing procedures because technology is always changing, and people change too, so it is imperative to keep updating systems as time goes on.

Using the buyer/seller checklist systems, I was able to move from making 13 sales in my first year to more than 53 sales the next year. The reason for the big jump in numbers was that I now had these systems in place, and I was able to hire my first full-time administrative person.

I delegated all of the non-sales functions—installing signs, inputting to the Multiple Listing Service, mailings and paperwork—to my newly hired assistant. I kept my focus on the four top-dollar productive activities that I wanted to concentrate on, which were: listing homes, selling homes, negotiating contracts, and prospecting two hours a day for new clients. Everything else, I delegated to my assistant.

My administrative person worked for me for about a year and a half and did a great job. I saw a quantum leap in my business. Then she decided to go into the real estate business herself, and I was left without an assistant. I hired a good friend whom I had known from the administrative department at Prudential and started from scratch. The mistake I had made with my first assistant was not documenting what we did. I didn't have an operations manual in place and, as a result, that former employee held me hostage in a sense. I didn't even know the passwords to get onto certain websites. I didn't know how to handle different procedures that our vendors required of us.

I decided I needed to create an operations manual and sat down with my new hire and went through everything. Together, we examined every process step by step, and then my new assistant would type it up. The next time a task had to be done, she could do it herself without my having to show her. Having this manual in place helped us grow even further.

I jumped from 53 sales to more than 77 sales the next year. This is when I hired two buyer agents to work for me, and the buyer agents knew exactly what they needed to do. They too had certain systems in place, from meeting with the customer to putting a contract together. It was a really great process from the beginning straight to the property closing.

My business continued to grow from there. I went from an individual agent office to a small team business to a much larger team. I hired a listing specialist, a courier to put signs out, a photographer to take pictures, and a bookkeeper to take care of the financing.

I actually hired the bookkeeper early on and put routines in place so that there was a set process for each check that came in. It was deposited in the bank on time, and had five days to clear. Once it cleared, then I was able to provide checks to the other agents on the team.

My administrative staff appreciates the operations manual because it makes their jobs a lot easier when the processes are followed. As my agents follow these steps, they also like it because they are able to leverage their time more efficiently. Those who don't follow the systems are the agents that I find struggle with time management and waste a lot of time. They are constantly repeating actions over and over again. If you do any tasks more than once, then you need a system in place for it.

You can take a look at some of my checklists as a starting point (check out www.freewilliestuff.com), but everyone's office is run differently. That is why I think there is no real cookie-cutter system. I think every agent must create his or her own operations manual, even if it is just a three-ring binder at the onset. If you take the time to set it up right the first time, you will avoid headaches and loss of business in the future.

Having all those systems in place not only permitted us to make our business run smoother, but they also generated a lot of repeat and referral business. Many agents tend to forget about the client once they receive the commission check and never reach out or talk to that client again because they feel that their job is done.

I believe that that is just when my job is beginning because I know that 65 or 70 percent of my future business will come from repeat and referral business. But you need a system in place for that as well, and so I developed the 29 Touch System.

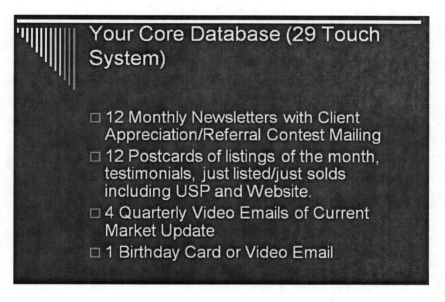

Your Core Database (29 Touch System)

- ☐ 12 Monthly Newsletters with Client Appreciation/Referral Contest Mailing
- ☐ 12 Postcards of listings of the month, testimonials, just listed/just solds including USP and Website.
- ☐ 4 Quarterly Video Emails of Current Market Update
- ☐ 1 Birthday Card or Video Email

With the 29 Touch System, that customer will receive 12 monthly newsletters in the mail. They will also have 12 postcards sent out to them, whether it is a "Just Listed" or "Just Sold" postcard. In addition, they will get one birthday call or email from me and they will receive four quarterly video market updates giving them good information on how the market is doing.

Here's the 29 Touch System:

- • 12 newsletters +

- 12 postcards +

- 1 birthday greeting +

- 4 video market updates = 29 touches from our company each year.

It is a proven system that allows us to stay top of mind with our clients. It has consistently generated a steady stream of repeat and referral business.

Whether you are a single agent, a small team, a big team, or a broker, as I have been every step of the way, it is important for you to have the proper systems in place in order to deliver quality, consistent service to your clients and keep gaining that repeat and referral business. I strongly urge any agent in the real estate business today to start off with just one process that they do over and over again. Develop that system, document it, and put it into an operations manual so that any person you hire in the future will be able to do exactly what you do and deliver reliable results to your customers as well.

CHAPTER 10

. . . . ———— . . . .

FINANCES: THE BUSINESS OF SUCCESS

Early on, I talked about the three important components to any successful business. The example I used was that of a three-legged stool, where one of the legs represented sales and marketing, the second leg represented operations, and the third leg, finance. All three legs of that stool must be balanced in order for your business to thrive.

Too many times, I have seen real estate agents make a lot of money in this business and then spend more than they actually make. I have seen more agents fail in this business—some going bankrupt or others being forced out of the business because they didn't know how to manage their finances. They either didn't have the background or the accountability to ensure that they were handling their finances correctly in order to be able to get through the good and bad cycles of any real estate market.

My first job with Prudential was in sales, but my paychecks were paid to me over a 13-week pay period. So whether I had a big commission check or a small commission check didn't matter; I was paid one-thirteenth of that. That worked out very well for me because, if there were weeks that I didn't have any commission checks coming in, I still knew that I had a steady paycheck. I was a W2 employee receiving health benefits and having taxes taken out of my check.

In 1995 when I went out on my own as an entrepreneur and a self-employed employee with Allstate Insurance Company, I went into it without any experience or knowledge of how to manage my finances and taxes. My first few years I didn't make a lot of money because most of my income was being invested back into my business.

But within three years, I found myself more than $125,000 in debt as a result of using business loans and credit card debt to support my Allstate business. Remember, this is what pushed me into the real estate business; I needed a part-time job in order to pay my personal bills, because all the money I was making in the insurance business was being invested back in to grow it.

As I recounted, I did fairly well in real estate, growing my sales from 13 homes to 77 homes in three years. I was able to pay back most of the debt that I owed. But on April 13, 1998, two days before taxes were due, I got a phone call from my accountant. He said, "Willie, congratulations. You had a great year last year, and I'm proud of all your accomplishments. That's the good news. The bad news is that you didn't pay enough in your estimated taxes because we based them on your prior year, and you've been so busy that you haven't been able to meet with me to give me updates on this year." He was right. In fact, I had gone almost a whole year without speaking with him at all. He said, "You owe the IRS about $76,000. I hope you saved some of that money that you made." I was taken back and felt that something had to be wrong—that my accountant had to be wrong. I met with him and we went over all the numbers, but he was right, everything was right. It just didn't seem fair. I felt like I had worked so hard and finally pulled myself out of debt, and now that I was making some profit, I had to give it all back to the government. Fortunately, I had that money in my account because I had started to build up reserves, but those reserves were diminished quickly by paying all those back taxes.

I vowed that year that I would start educating myself on financial management. I had some good discussions with my accountant and set up my business properly moving forward, because at this point it wasn't about breaking even or making a minimal amount. I was starting to do very well with my real estate business, and my insurance business was also going strong.

My accountant recommended that I hire a part-time bookkeeper, which would help me keep all of my expenses organized. The reason I didn't do my quarterly estimates properly was simply lack of time. I was working so much that all of my receipts were just thrown into a big cardboard box under my desk.

I gave that box of receipts to my new bookkeeper, and she just laughed and said, "Don't worry. We're going to get you straightened out." She started by looking at all of my receipts and taking stock of where I was. She looked at all my expenses and the income coming in and said that part of my problem was that all my business expenses were commingled with my personal credit cards and personal checking accounts.

The first thing that we did was set up a separate business account. I only used this for business expenses, and I opened a credit card that also was only used for the business. This kept my personal and business accounts separate. She then advised me, "Don't use cash. Always use your credit card so that we can manage and track your expenses." There had been a lot of cash expenses in the past that I just forgot about or didn't have a receipt for. I probably paid more in back taxes to the government than I really needed to do, but I couldn't show the write-offs.

My accountant recommended that I take 25 percent of each and every check I received, and put it away in a tax account. In the past if I received a check for $5,000, I would just take that $5,000 and spend it on myself or invest back into my business. That was a big mistake, and it's why I fell short on my estimates that year.

Now, that same $5,000 check gets deposited into my business account and $1,250 gets transferred into a tax account. Then I started paying myself a salary to my personal account. So I knew I had to stay within a certain budget. Having a budget set up is key; start with your personal budget first.

It took me a few weeks to do that, because to set up a budget I had to go back and track every penny that I spent. I recorded it into a software program. The program that I use and recommend today is QuickBooks. QuickBooks is an easy program to use, and you can purchase it inexpensively. I tried not to use any cash at all. Everything was purchased with a credit card. Any time I bought stamps, paid for advertising, or took a client out for a meal, I put it on the credit card. I saw very quickly where all of my money was going. Once you know where your money is going, you can become a better spender of your money. It makes a big difference.

As you fine-tune that home budget, you will have a better idea of how much income you need to generate from your business. In my situation, let's use $5,000 as a hypothetical. Five thousand dollars a month is what I needed to pay all my household expenses, rent, heat, lights, groceries, etc. That meant I had to take home $60,000 a year, but I also needed to plan for insurance, taxes, and my retirement on top of that amount.

Moving over to the business category, once I knew how much I needed to make for my home budget, then I went ahead and put together a business budget. I entered all the expenses that I had as far as advertising costs, broker fees, auto, gas, and cell phone, etc. This took me a few weeks to get down. The best way to do that, again, is to track every penny that you spend. I recommend going back 12 months through all your expenses and taking an average per month. So if I spent $6,000 in newspaper advertising annually, then I would need to plan $500 a month in my business budget for that expense. That's how I developed my business budget.

By having a business budget and a home budget, I now knew exactly how much income I needed to make in order to be successful in growing my business. Hiring a bookkeeper and getting all those systems in place allowed me to get a grip on my finances and move in the right direction.

In the early 2000s, there was an article in the *Wall Street Journal* ranking the top success factors for millionaires. These factors included being very disciplined, being honest with people, getting along with people, having a supportive spouse, working harder than most people, having a competitive personality, being well-organized, making wise investments, and the last one was "knowing their numbers." Above everything else, you had to know how to live within your means.

For years I carried that article with me, and I would refer to it every once in a while. I applied a lot of those success factors to my own business and personal life. I have always been very disciplined with my work. I set my work schedule up as if I had a 9–5 job. I am always honest with people and have always gotten along with people. I can sleep well at night because I know I have always taken care of my customers. I truly do love insurance and real estate, and now being able to help agents grow their business has become the icing on the cake for me.

As a result of that, I have developed strong leadership qualities, coaching and training agents all over the country. I have become very organized, and being able to see every check that is written out of my account and looking at my finances all in one place has taught me to know my numbers.

I have seen far too many agents in this business, when they start making good money in real estate, buy Rolex watches and $5,000 suits, lease expensive cars, and buy McMansions. The truth is, the real estate market is very seasonal and unpredictable. When times are good, they are very good, but when times are bad, they are really bad. You have to be prepared for both markets. Unfortunately, some very good real estate agents lose everything because they didn't do the proper planning. They weren't organized, they didn't live within their means, and, as a result of that, they are no longer in the business.

Here are some tips that I give to my agents and coaching members to make sure they have financial systems in place, like the home and business budgets I just mentioned:

- Have an adequate life insurance policy and a disability insurance policy to protect you and your loved ones.

- Create a will. Most people don't think about that, but once you have a family, it is important to have a will.

- Set up an automatic withdrawal into your savings account so you can build reserves. You should have at least one month worth of expenses as a reserve. I don't care if you save $50 or $100 or $500, but you must put money aside every month. Pay it as a bill to yourself. Pay it as a bill just like you pay your electric bill, your rent bill, your car bill, or your insurance bill, and don't look back. Don't have easy access to it, and that money will grow for you so that eventually you will have a large cash reserve. Ideally, you should have anywhere between three to six months of personal expense reserves set aside so that if times do get tough, or if there is a month or two where business is slow, you are able to continue paying your bills and keep your business going until things turn around again.

- Set up a retirement plan. There are various retirement plans out there, and I advise checking with your accountant. 401(k)s are an option. IRAs, Roth IRAs, or even SEP plans (simplified employee pension plan) are all good ways to get started.

- Make sure that you do a personal financial statement each year. Look at what assets you have and what liabilities you have. Completing that statement was a big eye-opener for me. I was making a lot of money, but I had significant debts as well. I was surprised to find myself with a negative net worth back in the late 1990s. My first step was getting out of the red, out of debt, and moving toward my net worth goal of $1 million or more. By completing that personal financial statement annually and setting up goals for myself, I was able to become debt free, and create six months of reserves not only for my personal expenses, but also for my business expenses. That is still true today. I have no debt in either one of my businesses and have very little personal debt.

What I recommend for agents who are used to working a 9–5 job and getting paid every two weeks is to start their business on a 13-week goal so that every quarter they know how much money they have moving into the next quarter.

In the real estate world, we sometimes get commission checks for $3,000, $5,000, and even up to $10,000 or more. I would deposit all my commissions into my business account, keeping my same monthly salary of $5,000 a month. There may have been some months that I made $15,000–$20,000 in commissions, but I still remained disciplined and only took out $5,000 a month for my home expenses. Everything else stayed in the business account.

At the end of the year, I would sit down with my accountant and pay all my taxes. Whatever was left, in essence my profit, I would treat as a bonus. So every year I would get a bonus. Sometimes that bonus would be pretty significant. I would take it and put more money aside for retirement. Or I would use that bonus to put more money toward a personal debt that I might have had. Or I would take that bonus to take a family trip or upgrade a vehicle. But if I had spent that money along the way—if one month I had made $15,000 and decided to spend it on a luxurious trip, and then the next month I didn't make any commissions—I would have ended up borrowing money from my credit card to pay my mortgage, and you can see how very quickly you can get yourself in big financial trouble by doing that.

The key to success on the financial side, and a lesson learned, is that you must pay yourself a consistent salary and run your business like a business, knowing that every penny you *make* is not necessarily yours to *spend*. It has to be allocated properly so that you are paying your other obligations and are able to withstand the ups and downs of the real estate business.

Why is it that some agents who make $250,000 in gross commission income end up keeping $200,000 of that for their personal income, while other agents who make $2 million in commissions actually lose money at the end of the year?

I have found from coaching agents all across the country that the smart agents are the ones who really know their numbers, track their expenses, and make a good profit at the end of the year. The agents who are doing four or five times the business of any other agent and lose money every year—those are the agents who find themselves out of business. The simple reason is because they didn't have financial systems in place, didn't know their numbers, didn't track their expenses, and didn't have a reserve set up for themselves.

The reason I recommend that agents really push toward getting six months' worth of expenses in reserve is because, as real estate agents, we work on a 90-day cycle. If I take you out today to show you a home, it may take me three to four weeks of showing you properties before you decide what home you actually want to buy. Then once you put a contract on that home, it may take another six to eight weeks to close. So just because you have a buyer today, it could still be another 90 days before you get a paycheck. That is why it is so important to build up your reserves.

If I happen to have a very soft quarter, and I have to go through three months of reserves because I wasn't getting a check or because things were slow, I have to turn things around pretty quickly. I have an additional 90 days to do that or I will be in hot water and out of business.

Not having the right financial systems in place can be detrimental to any business, causing you to go bankrupt or lose your business altogether. That is why I titled this book, *How To Avoid Getting Your Ass Kicked In The Real Estate Business*, because these are key systems that need to be set up and taken very seriously from the beginning. I wish I knew what I know now back when I first started. I would have hired a bookkeeper a lot sooner. I would have known my numbers more thoroughly, and I would have kept a monthly profit and loss statement. I also would have created reserves as soon as I could.

But the one thing I see a lot of agents neglect today is that they don't put money back into their business. My advice is that you should cut your home expenses *before* you cut your business expenses. Perhaps you don't go to Starbucks every day. Perhaps you pack a lunch instead of going out to lunch every day. Perhaps you only go out to eat once a week instead of five times a week. The list goes on and on. You want to make your cuts at home first before you start cutting back on your business, because your business is the golden goose laying the golden egg, which is that commission check. You want your business to serve you. You don't want to be serving your business. So it is very important that you get that business cranking and producing the money that it needs to make. Once you start building up a reserve and have bigger bonuses at the end of the year based on your profits, then you can do the extra things that you want to do on a personal level. I encourage agents to make sure that they are investing back into their business.

When things are going good, things go well, but when the business starts to slow down, the first thing I see agents do is start making reductions in their business budget. They start cutting their advertising expenses. Let me state this again, investing in lead generation is the most important expense that you will have on your books, so treat those advertising costs as an investment. It is an investment back into your business. It is not an expense. If you have to put those investments on a credit card, that's okay. It is a good debt. It is how I funded my business in the beginning. When the business comes in, you can pay off the debt as I did.

What you don't want to put on a credit card are snowmobiles or boats or any other depreciating assets that are personal items and are not investments back into your business. The money that I spend on credit cards is to grow my business. Most agents just don't put enough money back into their business.

I advise every agent that I work with to put 10 percent of their income back into their marketing and advertising budget. So if you want to make $100,000 a year, then you need to budget $10,000 to invest back into advertising and marketing in order to achieve that goal. I guarantee that if you put that money back into the right places, especially if you invest it into the four lead generation pillars that I mentioned earlier in the book, you will continue to grow your business, and it will be money well spent.

My motto has always been that fortune cookie my daughter Christine opened up for me back in 2002. "The road to success is always under construction." You never know when you really hit the true meaning of success. I think that is why I work so hard, to keep improving all the time. I never settle for the status quo. I am always looking to find a better way.

My hope is I will save people who read this book from making a lot of the same mistakes that I have made, of not having a good financial system in place, of not having separate bank accounts, of not hiring a bookkeeper. I know that if I had done these things earlier in my career I would have been even more successful today. I would have more money in the bank, more money in my retirement accounts, and I wouldn't have overspent on things that didn't work. I didn't know how to measure their ROI (return on investment), like the $12,000 I spent on a billboard. I thought it was great because everyone said they saw it, but when I looked at the numbers, I was only able to track only one or two sales to it.

If you are a real estate agent and you follow just some of the models and systems mentioned in this book, you *will* avoid getting your ass kicked in the real estate business, and instead you will go on to enjoy a very profitable and successful career just as I have.

Download a free copy of a Personal Financial Statement and a Profit and Loss Statement at: www.freewilliestuff.com.

PERSONAL FINANCIAL STATEMENT

Date Received ....

By .... Vamshi Reddy ....

Section 1-Individual Information		Section 2-Other Party Information	
Name		Name	
Address		Address	
City, State, Zip		City, State, Zip	
Position or Occupation		Position or Occupation	
Employer's Name		Employer's Name	
Employer's Address		Employer's Address	
City, State, Zip		City, State, Zip	
Res. Phone	Bus. Phone	Res. Phone	Bus. Phone
Social Security No.	Date of Birth	Social Security No.	Date of Birth

Financial Condition as of

Please Do Not Leave Any Questions Unanswered. Use "No" or "None" Where Necessary

Assets (do not include assets of doubtful value)	In dollars (omit cents)	Liabilities	In dollars (omit cents)
Cash on hand (See Schedule A)		Notes Payable to Banks - Secured (See Schedule H)	
Cash in other Banks (See Schedule A) Escrow		Notes payable to Banks - Unsecured (see Schedule H)	
Listed Securities (See Schedule B)		Amounts Payable to Others (See Schedule H)	
Unlisted Securities (See Schedule C)		Due to Brokers (See Schedule H)	
Partial Interest in Real Estate Equities (See Schedule D)		Accounts and Bills Due	
Real Estate Owned (See Attached document)		Real Estate Mortgages Payable (See Schedule D & E)	-
Accounts, Loans, Notes, Mort. Receivable(See Schedule F)		Unpaid Income Tax	
Vehicles		Other Unpaid Taxes and Interest	
Cash Value - Life Insurance (See Schedule G)		Loans on Life Insurance Policies (See Schedule G)	
Other Assets - Itemize		Other Debts - Itemize: See Schedule H)	
		Accounts Payables	
		Total Liabilities	$ -
		Net Worth	$ -
Total Assets	$ -	Total Liabilities and Net Worth	$ -
Annual Income For Year Ended 2004	Amounts	Contingent Liabilities	Amounts
Salary	+	Contingent Liabilities? (as endorser, co-maker or guarantor)	
Bonus & Commissions		On leases? On contracts?	
Dividends		Involvement in pending legal actions?	
Real Estate Income		Other special debt or circumstances?	
Other Income - You need not disclose income derived from alimony, child support, and/or separate maintenance, unless you desire the bank to consider that income in their determination of whether or not they will grant you the credit requested.		Contested income tax liens?	
		If yes to any question's), describe:	
Total	$ -	Total Contingent Liabilities	$ -

The financial statement and the information contained herein is given to the lender, by the undersigned for the purpose of inducing the Lender, from time to time, to extend credit to or otherwise become or remain the creditor of the undersigned, or persons, firms or corporations in whose behalf the undersigned may either individually or jointly with others, execute a guarantee in the Lender's favor. The undersigned acknowledges that the Lender will rely on the information contained in this Financial Statement in making it: credit decision, and under penalty of perjury, represents and warrants that such information is true and complete and that there are no material omissions. The undersigned agrees that the Lender may consider this financial statement as continuing to be true and complete until a written notice of a change is given to the Lender by the undersigned. The lender is authorized to make all inquiries that it deems necessary to verify the accuracy of the information contained herein and to determine the undersigned's creditworthiness. The Lender is further authorized to respond to any inquiries from others concerning the Lender's credit experience with the undersigned.

Date _____ Signed: _____ (Applicant)

Date _____ Signed: _____ (Co-Applicant)

YEAR	PROFIT & LOSS STATEMENT

INCOME	
GROSS SALES	
LESS RETURNS	
LESS DISCOUNTS	
LESS BAD DEBTS	
INTEREST, RENT AND ROYALTIES	
TOTAL INCOME	
EXPENSES	
COST OF GOODS SOLD	
DIRECT PAYROLL	
INDIRECT PAYROLL	
TAXES, OTHER THAN INCOME TAX	
SALES EXPENSES	
SHIPPING AND POSTAGE	
ADVERTISING AND PROMOTION	
OFFICE EXPENSES	
TRAVEL AND ENTERTAINMENT	
PHONE	
OTHER UTILITIES	
AUTOMOBILE	
INSURANCE	
PROFESSIONAL FEES	
RENT	
INTEREST ON LOANS	
OTHER, MISC.	
TOTAL EXPENSES	
NET INCOME	
LESS INCOME TAX	
NET INCOME AFTER TAX	

ACKNOWLEDGMENTS

I would like to thank all of the role models and mentors I have sought advice from and learned so much from over the years. I would also like to thank all of my awesome agents, staff, and coaching members who are with me today and those in the past who have helped me succeed. And lastly, I would like to thank my family and close friends who have always been patient with me and have supported me in everything I have ever done. My business and personal life would not have been the same without all of the people above that I mentioned. No names needed … you all know who you are!

AUTHOR BIO

Willie Miranda has more than twenty-four years of experience in the real estate and insurance industry. Willie has worked with hundreds of real estate agents across the country to help market and promote their real estate services to their clients through better marketing communications and systems. Under his leadership, several real estate agents and brokers have grown their personal relationships with their clients, resulting in a more profitable repeat and referral business for those that have followed Willie's referral and real estate systems. Willie is the president and founder of Miranda Real Estate Group, Inc., an award-winning real estate brokerage headquartered in Clifton Park, NY, specializing in residential and commercial real estate. Willie is also the president and owner of Miranda Insurance Agency, Inc. that is associated with the Allstate Insurance Corporation.

Willie has been married to his wife Shari since 1993, and they have two daughters, Christine (18) and Julia (15). Willie enjoys family time, coaching his kids in sports, and giving back to various nonprofit organizations in his community such as The Children's Hospital at Albany Medical Center.

CPSIA information can be obtained at www.ICGtesting.com
Printed in the USA
LVOW10s1055061215

465613LV00033B/1009/P